THE
UNEXPECTED
COP

D0817093

THE
UNEXPECTED
COP

INDIAN ERNIE ON A
LIFE OF LEADERSHIP

ERNIE LOUTTIT

University of Regina Press

Printed and bound in Canada at Friesens. The text of this book is printed on 100% post-consumer recycled paper with earth-friendly vegetable-based inks.

Cover design: Duncan Campbell, University of Regina Press
Text design: John van der Woude, JVDW Designs
Copy editor: Kirsten Craven
Proofreader: Rhonda Kronyk
Cover photo: William Hamilton, Hamilton Photographics

Library and Archives Canada Cataloguing in Publication
Ernie, 1961-, author
    The unexpected cop : Indian Ernie on a life of leadership / Ernie Louttit.

Issued in print and electronic formats.
ISBN 978-0-88977-599-2 (softcover).—ISBN 978-0-88977-600-5 (PDF).—ISBN 978-0-88977-601-2 (HTML)

1. Louttit, Ernie, 1961-. 2. Saskatoon (Sask.). Police Service.
3. Police—Saskatchewan—Saskatoon—Biography. 4. Native peoples—Saskatchewan—Saskatoon—Biography. 5. Community leadership.
6. Autobiographies. I. Title.

HV7911.L698A3 2019   363.2092   C2018-906034-4   C2018-906035-2
10 9 8 7 6 5 4 3 2

University of Regina Press, University of Regina
Regina, Saskatchewan, Canada, S4S 0A2
tel: (306) 585-4758 fax: (306) 585-4699
web: www.uofrpress.ca

We acknowledge the support of the Canada Council for the Arts for our publishing program. We acknowledge the financial support of the Government of Canada. / Nous reconnaissons l'appui financier du gouvernement du Canada. This publication was made possible with support from Creative Saskatchewan's Book Publishing Production Grant Program.

*To people who read because they want and like
to. To the librarians, educators, and people who
make books a part of young people's lives. To
the people who publish books, and to the many
organizations who support literacy in Canada.*

*To the people who guard, provide care for, and protect
my family and my country every day, 24/7/365, often
at a hidden and sometimes visible cost to themselves.*

*To my wife Christine and our children, all the
members of our two families, and to my mother
Hazel and my stepfather Jack, who gave me the
ideal place to finish this book: a cabin in northern
Ontario, built in the woods with their own labour.*

CONTENTS

PREFACE

We all remember good teachers. Teachers who were passionate and made learning fun. It is the same with strong and decisive leaders. People who changed things by their efforts and by the examples they set. We remember people who made a difference in our lives.

I was, and in many ways still am, in a profession where the raw material of my everyday life was people. People inspire me every day to try to be a better person. I was a police officer for almost thirty years, and I have seen a lot of what humanity has to offer, good and bad.

Before policing I was a soldier, and before that I was a kid growing up in northern Ontario. Since leaving policing, I have become a writer and public speaker. People inspired me to be passionate about leadership and writing. They have allowed me to share my views and perspectives with a larger audience than I could have imagined. It took nearly two years from when my first book was published for me to call myself a writer. I felt like more of a storyteller than a writer. Telling stories from my experiences was how I passed on knowledge.

This is my third book. You don't have to read the other two to read this one, though it would be nice if you did. For those readers who are back for the third time, you have my profound gratitude; it has been an honour and a privilege to have you read what I have written.

For those of you who are not familiar with me, I am a member of the Missanabie Cree First Nation. I live off reserve in Saskatoon, Saskatchewan. I am married with four grown children. I joined the Canadian Armed Forces in December 1978. I served in the infantry and military police until I joined the Saskatoon Police Service in January 1987.

When I was a police officer, I had a habit of leaving my patrol car and walking around in the poorest neighbourhoods when I didn't have a call. The local kids would follow me and, after asking my name, would ask if I was an Indian. Within a month or two, whenever I showed up, the kids would loudly exclaim, "It's Indian Ernie!" Eventually, everyone in the areas I worked was calling me "Indian Ernie," or variations on it, depending on which side of the law they were on. The name stuck with me for my entire career.

I left policing in October 2013 and wrote my first book, *Indian Ernie: Perspectives on Policing and Leadership*, which was released in November 2013. People are very passionate about policing and leadership, and not a day has gone by since I left where policing and leadership are not featured in a news headline. Policing and justice are emotional topics for a lot of people. Issues where policing and race intersect always start the water boiling.

I am using this opportunity to talk about many different and sometimes very difficult subjects. Sexual violence, fires, use of force by police, and gender inequality in policing, as well as leadership, all get a nod this time. Post-traumatic stress and advice on how to navigate contacts with police for Indigenous youth are here.

Some stories I have written are personal and some are almost editorial. I thought putting myself out there as a writer would get easier as I went along. In fact, it is the opposite: my fear that people will not be interested or engaged grows the more I write. But, like a moth to the flame, I am back. I hope you enjoy this and thank you for being here.

One of my first jobs at thirteen years old in the '70s was working at a small tourist camp on Cameron Lake, about a forty-five-minute journey on the Oba River with a sixteen-foot boat powered by a twenty-horsepower outboard motor. I did odd jobs like bringing supplies and cleaning up around the camps. It is a little camp located on a hill on the north side of the lake as you enter it. There are five cabins at the main site and one on another island across a channel, all built long before I worked there. It is still operating with a new owner to this day. I remember my mother would say, without fail every time I set out to go to the camp, "Watch out for the rocks son," and "Do you know where the rocks are?"

The Oba River is a small river cut into the Canadian Shield thousands of years ago. There are many large rocks below the surface of the water that an outboard motor can strike. There are some places where they break through to the surface, with original names like "first rocks," "second rocks," and "the shallows." It was a point of pride for all the men and aspiring men back then to know where the rocks were. To hit a rock and break your motor was to guarantee years of endless teasing, not to mention that you could lose your job. My first solo trip up the river was slow: it took me an hour and a half. I was admonished for wasting gas and taking too long when I got to the camp. Each trip afterwards my confidence grew, and I began making trips at all hours, even as dusk was setting in. I knew the rocks and had passed an important test in the eyes of northerners. There were still many things you had to be careful of on the river, like deadhead logs or fallen trees, but if you knew those damn rocks you were considered good to go.

For whatever reason, as I began writing this new book, this came to mind. We all do well if we know where the rocks are or what the rocks are. The men used to travel the river with us when we were children, but they never explained how they knew where the rocks were or took the time to point them out. You were expected to learn them as you went. In some places they would slow down if the river levels were low, but more often than not they would go through the rocks at full throttle. So you watched and learned. You learned where the bow of the boat pointed as you rounded a curve and where what appeared to be channels were. So many things in life are like rivers we have to navigate. In the beginning, unless someone helps to explain and teach you, those rivers can be scary and filled with unseen threats waiting to put a stop to your progress.

I have never been the type of person to let people tear down rivers without any knowledge if I have information to share about them. The Oba River had no signposts or navigational aids, so passing knowledge along to a newcomer meant the wisdom was based on experience and perspective.

It is the same with writing about policing, leadership, and race issues. The stories are from my perspectives and experiences, and my hope is they will help people look at some issues and see where the obstacles and challenges lie. The fundamentals of good leadership never change. What makes a good and healthy relationship between the police and the communities they serve is knowledge about what is being done to keep everyone safe and why it is done. Race issues diminish with tolerance, knowledge, and dialogue.

There are still unexpected obstacles like deadhead logs and fallen trees, but if you have an idea of where the rocks are you are better positioned to move ahead. I have learned something every day since I left policing. It is a whole new river now.

ACKNOWLEDGEMENTS

I am sitting in a screened enclosure called "Buzzy's bug hut" in Oba, northern Ontario, while writing my acknowledgements. I haven't seen anyone but my mother and my stepfather all day. In spite of that, I feel overwhelmed with gratitude to all the people who have contributed and given me the opportunity to write my third book.

First off, I would like to thank my wife Christine and our children for all of their love, support, and encouragement while I was two-finger typing the manuscript, transcribing it from my handwritten version.

I would like to thank all the readers of my first two books who asked me—at Sobeys, Walmart, Costco, Tim Hortons, or any other place they ran into me—when a new book was coming out. I would like to thank anyone new to me who is holding this book in their hands right now. Thanks for being readers, because readers are leaders.

All the organizations and groups who asked me to speak at their conferences or their libraries, allowing me to slip in the stories that later formed the basis of chapters in this book, deserve credit and acknowledgement as well. The Saskatchewan Indian Gaming Authority, Saskatchewan Emergency Medical Services Association, Saskatchewan Union of Nurses, University of Saskatchewan, Saskatchewan Police College, First Nations University of Canada (Prince Albert and Regina), and the Northern Lights School Division are just some of the organizations that have allowed me to continue in my new career.

The dedicated librarians of the communities of Meadow Lake, Saskatoon, Elrose, Kindersley, Dalmeny, Martensville, Aberdeen, Bruno, Humboldt, Viscount, Melfort, Waterous, Elbow, Dillon, and Canoe Lake who tracked me down to come and speak—even during harvest—at their libraries are amazing, community-minded people.

I would like to extend a special thank-you to the Hnatyshyn Foundation for selecting me as one of the 150 recipients of the REVEAL Indigenous Art Awards in May of 2017. The award allowed me to travel and continue writing with greater peace of mind. As well, I would like to thank all the private and government organizations who, through their contributions to the literary world, allow publishers to get books into the hands of readers.

We are blessed to live in a country with such freedom. Thank you to all the members of the military, first responders who protect us, corrections, and medical fields past and present who have given us the gifts of freedom, security, and peace of mind. I would like to thank all the leaders, whatever it is that you do, from law enforcement to education, who try to make our lives better every day.

Lastly, I would like to thank Bruce Walsh, Sean Prpick, and the University of Regina Press for all the work and energy they have expended to let me be heard.

I know I have missed someone, but it was not on purpose.

CHAPTER 1
SWEET TEA AND WOODSMOKE

I used to visit *Mooshom*, or Grandfather in Cree, at his tiny one-room log cabin on a rocky Canadian Shield hill that overlooked the graveyard and had a view of the Oba River. He was not my grandfather, nor was he Cree like me, but rather Ojibway, but that didn't seem to matter to either of us. My grandfather was killed in the Second World War. I was named after him. My grandfather on my mother's side died when I was young. We were actually on the train going to visit him when the conductor told my mother he had died. The town where I grew up in northern Ontario had about 120 people. Most people lived in the townsite, which was on both sides of the railway tracks, and there were only five occupied cabins or houses down by the river.

The river was a frequent destination for young people to fish or swim. Mooshom lived across from an older trapper who kept a dog team chained all around his property. He used those dogs right up until the early nineties and kept a couple even after he stopped using them as a dog team. The trapper's dogs were scary, straining at their chains and growling every time they scented you. When I was a boy, they scared me so much I always loaded up on rocks and carried a big stick in case they broke their chains.

The grandfather on the hill was a quiet man with a weathered face and dressed in heavy pants and shirts, regardless of the season. He had a gentle smile and a sadness about him that made me want to talk to him every time I saw him. Eventually, I worked up enough courage to take two pickerel I had caught to his cabin, braving the walk past the trapper's dog team. My heart pounding, I arrived at the safe zone in front of his cabin. He smiled and took the fish. He told me in his quiet voice that the trapper's dogs knew I was scared and that is why they barked like they did. He made tea for us in tin cups with evaporated milk and lots of sugar without ever asking if I wanted any. I supposed it was a given.

He didn't say much as we drank our tea. I was talking quite a bit, asking questions about what Oba was like when he was young. Finally, I stopped asking questions because his answers were so short. We sat in silence for a while and I thanked him for the tea. He told me quietly that I talked too much. I wasn't offended and left with a belly full of warm, sweet tea and a big smile. I wasn't as afraid as I walked past the trapper's snarling dogs. It was one of the most memorable visits I had with an Elder. We didn't use that term when I grew up, as I grew up off reserve. But I instinctively knew he was a special man.

I went back several times over the course of that summer and into the fall. I would bring fish or sometimes just a can of Carnation evaporated milk. We would drink tea in near silence, with the air rich with the smell of woodsmoke and the river. It was almost like I was absorbing his patience and wisdom without knowing it. I always felt wiser and braver when I left, and those damn dogs held no sway over me anymore. I strode down the hill on confident legs.

Unfortunately, I turned twelve during this period and discovered girls, even if they had not discovered me. I started working at a fishing camp and making money. My visits grew farther and farther apart until, except for the nod of my head as I went past his cabin, I didn't see him anymore. Of course, I didn't realize it then, or for many years afterwards, but I had lost my closest connection to learning traditional ways and had let so much knowledge slip away. I had lost touch with a man who could teach with an economy of words and simple knowing glances. I went on to go away for high school and eventually joined the army. He passed away while I was away, and there was so much I did not know about him. I suppose I could have asked other people about him, but in the end would it have changed the way I felt? Probably not.

A knowledge keeper maybe not in the strict traditional sense, the grandfather had taught me patience and to seek knowledge. There were others like my mother and regular teachers who encouraged me to learn and especially to read. None of them provided such a classroom, sweet tea, or a view of the river.

When I think of what was lost and what can still be gained or even recovered in traditional learning, I like to think our young people will be the champions of this new learning. Our Oral Tradition of storytelling is not threatened by the many new means of passing on traditions. It is, in fact, enhanced by all the new forms of media. It is faster, and the choices are vast. What we take from it will challenge how well we are grounded in what we value and believe.

There are many experiences we as First Nations people can pass on through our stories. There is no clear definition of who can be a storyteller, for that matter. There are periods of our time that can be divided into experiences, good and bad. There is no one alive who can pass on real time stories from pre-contact with Europeans; any stories from then have passed through many variations depending on the storyteller, so a grain of salt is necessary for our interpretations. Some storytellers colour those days as idyllic and free of troubles, while others paint a realistic gritty picture of the day-to-day struggles to survive. The truth lies somewhere in between, I would suspect.

The next period is the most difficult and spans several hundred years. The attempts by Europeans to dominate, eliminate, or assimilate First Nations present the biggest challenge to the keepers of our stories. So many have passed and many who remember are scarred and bitter. The past ten years have seen attempts at reconciliation and expressed regret, which our storytellers have to interpret somehow for the young people. I have never been much of a traditionalist. I can point to the army and my police work for this because we were so mission-driven in what we did. It doesn't mean I didn't listen to the stories. I knew their importance to all of us. There will always be new issues arising, but we will get there. We will emerge strong as always.

The next period is the present, when our storytellers are not defined as much by our age but rather by our experiences and our modern methods of telling our stories. I think I am on the edge of this last period and the start of the new one. I am getting closer to ordering from the senior's menu than I am to skipping over it.

I have always taught others by telling stories based on my experiences and observations. I am also utterly ruthless when I take positive leadership examples from others to tell stories and hopefully make people look to the future while respecting the past. I am putting my hand up to be considered a storyteller and keeping my ears open to hear others. For all young people my first words of advice are do not let the stories of the people who lived through the challenges you will eventually face get away without at least hearing how they coped and what they learned. What you take away may surprise you.

CHAPTER 2
WHERE THERE'S SMOKE—
THE POWER OF FIRE

I grew up in a small town called Oba in northern Ontario. Oba is on the northern edge of the Canadian Shield, sixty-four kilometres from the next community and surrounded by forests. Two railroads and a bush road connect it with the rest of the world. In the early 1970s there were about a hundred people living there in mostly wooden houses, heating them with either wood or oil. Many of the homes were built in the thirties and forties with no government inspections or fire safety standards utilized. Any sign of smoke coming from anything other than a known source would immediately fill you with apprehension. There was no firefighting equipment, and as a teenager I never asked if there was any kind of plan in the case of a fire. Forest fires seemed to be the biggest threat, but no one ever spoke about them and it seemed never uttering the words was the best prevention.

There were several businesses in Oba: two hotels, the railway station, and the flagship general store. I don't know when it was built. I suspect it was in the thirties. It was a beautiful, solid, three-story structure with hardwood floors throughout. When I was a boy, I would marvel at all the beautiful things the store owners displayed. It had just about everything you could want. A post office, clothing, food, and a meat counter. The post office was my favourite place. It was my connection with the outside world. Behind the store was a large warehouse. Even back then in the seventies, the warehouse had so many antiques it would have been a dream find for the pickers you see now on various television programs. Behind the warehouse was a diesel generator housed in a small shed. The diesel generator provided electricity to the store in the years before the government built a power generating station. In the expansive yard of the store, barrels of gas, oil, and propane tanks were stacked and ready for sale. The store also sold guns and ammunition. The store went through a couple of owners when I was growing up, but it always seemed viable and an anchor in the community.

In 1976 the store was sold to a new owner who moved there with his wife and three children. Shortly after they took over, on a beautiful summer day, a plume of gray smoke emerged from the area of the diesel shed. Several people spotted it at the same time, including me, and we all went forward to investigate. The diesel shed had been saturated with lubricants, spilled diesel, and other flammables over the years, and it quickly became fully engulfed in flames. I ran to the hotel to tell everyone and to the railway station to see if there was anything there to fight the fire with.

At the station there was a single fire hose the station agent used to clean the tractor and baggage wagons, but the water pressure was so inadequate it was useless. It has been forty years since the fire, yet many of my memories are still quite vivid—I knew I wanted to help. I don't remember who suggested it, but someone said to start rolling the barrels of gas out of the fire's path. In retrospect, a near suicidal undertaking at fifteen years old, although it seemed like a good idea at the time.

The fire quickly spread to the old wooden warehouse and sparks and embers were flying up into the air and landing all over the tinderbox town and surrounding forest. The yard where the gas and diesel barrels were piled had long ago been saturated by spills and leaks. One of the men told me to get the hell out of there. The intense heat had reached one of the many propane tanks and caused one of the melt plugs to go. Melt plugs are safety values that melt to prevent a propane tank from exploding like a bomb. The gas shoots out like a flame-thrower, and it makes a terrifying screech like a constant high-pitched scream.

The mournful sound increased as the heat and flames reached other propane tanks. Soon the fire had the store and it began to burn. The barrels of gas and oil had no such safety features and began to blow up, flying through the air and landing across the railway tracks, starting a fire in the bush. The look of dismay and shock on everyone's faces was something I will never forget. Through the smoke and haze I could see people crying and standing helpless, with no equipment to fight the fire at all. I don't remember any clear leader emerging while the fire took the heart of the town, but I was just a kid, so I might have missed it.

The forest fire prompted the Ministry of Natural Resources to send a water bomber to start attacking the flames. A couple of hours into the fire, a ministry truck and firefighters arrived. They didn't stop at the store fire and went to fight the forest fire. My brother and I were given the task of standing guard on the roof of our house with buckets of water to extinguish any embers that landed there.

In frustration, my mother went to the river and took one of the pumps the ministry firefighters were using to fight the forest fire. The firefighters came back to the site of the store and recovered it. No charges were laid because the firefighters understood the theft of their pump was an emotional response to the tragedy. My mother was always a leader, though a bit of a rebellious one during this incident. Eventually, the store and all the outbuildings were consumed by the flames and the most intense period of danger passed. Miraculously, no one was killed or seriously injured during the fire, and as the day ended everyone was thankful for that one small mercy.

The town recovered from its shock and sadness. The owners built a new store and carried on until Oba shrank so much it was no longer a workable venture. By then, I was long gone and in the army. The Oba general store fire was my first date in a reluctant relationship I have had with fires and arson.

My next date with fire occurred when I was in the army. One summer it was announced we were going to do a ceremony known as troop the colour. Basically, it was a public parade where we marched the regimental colours or flags to celebrate our regiment's anniversary. An old tradition from the days when the colours or flags of a regiment were the rallying points on a battlefield, the trooping of the colours was performed so every soldier knew what to look for in the smoke and haze. It was a big deal. We had to practice drill for several weeks before the occasion. The whole thing was a lot of work, but it was part of instilling pride in ourselves and in the regiment. Part of the celebrations required us to fill thousands of sandbags and rec-reate bunkers in the drill hall. The bunkers were ordained with camouflage nets and dim lighting. It was to recreate what it was like in the First World War trench system without all the mud and blood. It was to be a 24/7 bar. As we were hosting veter-ans and former members of the regiment, it was meant to be a social centre of the week-long celebration of the trooping of the colours. It was called the "Better 'Ole," named after an expression from the First World War when soldiers complained about their trench and the reply would be, "If you know of a better hole, go to it."

The parade took place in Assiniboine Park, in the heart of Winnipeg, and seemed to go off without a hitch. After the parade was over, the battalion and our guests deployed to the Better 'Ole. The beer was cheap and flowed freely. After a while it began to look like a First World War battlefield as soldiers passed out over sandbags and slept in corners. We were in about the thirty-sixth hour of our deployment and it was very early in the morning when our NCOs (noncommissioned officers) came in and told us we were deploying to fight forest fires in northern Manitoba and to be ready to go in two hours.

There was a mad rush to shower, pack our kit, and drink as much coffee as possible before reporting to our respective companies. We were deploying to a town called Bissett, Manitoba. During all the celebrations we obviously had not been keeping track of the local news. The forest fire situation in northern Manitoba was getting out of hand, and the fires were threatening the town. We were loaded up in the back of 2 1/2-ton trucks, where we sat on wooden benches. My platoon slept most of the way in the back of the deuce and a half, stinking of stale beer.

When we arrived at the town and deployed, I marvelled at the smoothness of the operation. The battalion that had been totally dedicated to party for the remainder of the week had sorted itself out in a couple of hours. We were cohesive and committed. The smell of burning forests always made me apprehensive and created a feeling of uncertainty. My job was to mostly fight spot fires with a metal tank of water strapped to my back and a shovel. It was hot and sweaty work. Your throat and eyes were always irritated. There were a couple of operational firsts for me: deploying from a helicopter to fight spot fires, and driving armoured personal carriers in the forest. The front line-trained firefighters took on the main fires and we had the manpower to deal with everything else.

Within a couple of days, the fires were under control and we redeployed to garrison. While we were gone, the rear party had taken down our Better 'Ole and we resumed our normal duties. We used to practise bug out drills. When the unit was in garrison, periodically they would practise short notice deployment. The forest fires were the first real ones I had taken part in. If there was a worst-case scenario for a rapid deployment, this was it. A 24/7 bar and the majority of the battalion being off duty and encouraged to celebrate did not make for the most deployment-ready unit. It was a good lesson for me. For all of the fun I was having in the army, it could at any moment get serious.

When I was a police officer, people would often say to me, "I could never do your job. It's too sad." I would say the same thing to firefighters. I know all the jokes and banter about the relationship between firefighters and the police. I have even made a few snide remarks over the years about firefighters and their workload. The experiences I have had over the course of my career have imbedded a deep respect for firefighters and fire investigators. The training and discipline required to be a firefighter is as intense as any trade I've seen. When it is go time, and a fire is in progress, these men and women give it their all.

Shortly after graduating from the Saskatchewan Police College, I went to my first house fire in Saskatoon. My partner and I arrived before the firefighters, which was often the case because we drove cars and they drove trucks. I don't recall receiving very much information about fires and proper police response to fires from police college. When we arrived at the fire, I saw a modern-looking two-story home in flames. The neighbours didn't know if anyone was home.

My partner and I rushed to the front door and opened it. The superheated air and visible flames immediately forced us out. The frustration of being unable to go in, as well as the fear the force of the fire caused, made me glad to see the trucks arriving. My corporal told us after he arrived to leave the firefighting to the firefighters but not a lot else. I watched as the firefighters quickly deployed and attacked the fire. Disciplined and well-orchestrated tactics and teamwork saved the home, albeit heavily damaged. Dealing with fires and my role as a police officer at the scenes were apparently things I would have to learn on the go.

As the years went by, I did traffic control at fire scenes and was basically a spectator at numerous fires. The real interaction took place at accident scenes and medical emergencies. Like all professional relationships, more interaction increases respect and communication, and I was proud to count many firefighters as my friends. Still, at the upper levels there seemed to be a strained relationship between all first responders as each service vied for an ever-changing slice of the municipal budget for equipment and training.

I took the next step in my relationship with fires in October 1996. I was terrible at taking time off in a timely matter as required by the police contract, so my staff sergeant ordered me to take off a day shift. I had no court appearances and I didn't like taking night shifts off, so I didn't protest. It was a pleasant fall day as I stepped into the backyard to drink my coffee. I saw a large plume of black smoke rising from the west. The old and familiar feeling of apprehension was immediate. I knew instinctively there was a major fire. Our children were very young in 1996—five, three, and almost two years old—so my wife was happy I was home to help her that day. I told her something big was happening downtown and, as it was my platoon working, I was going to call in and see if I was needed. My wife rolled her eyes as we had been down this road before.

I called the staff sergeant and he stated a major furniture store was on fire in the downtown and every available unit was committed. He reluctantly agreed to let me come in. I told my wife and promised I would make it up to her for leaving. The building was fully engulfed and was easily one of the most visually spectacular fires I have ever seen as I drove into the downtown. When I arrived at the station, I reported in and was told to go see the staff sergeant in the major crimes section.

Puzzled, I went there. I was expecting to take calls for service as a uniformed patrol officer, as everyone was tied up at the fire. When I reported, the staff sergeant quickly explained he had no available investigators. The investigation of the fire was mine until an investigator was available. I had one suit and it wasn't even a nice one. I knew next to nothing about fire investigation, and science wasn't one of my strong points. I didn't really have a clue where to start, so I just said, "Yes, sir." He gave me a quick briefing on what he knew so far and away I went, back home to put on a suit and gather my thoughts before heading to the fire scene. I didn't know the exact cost of the building and its contents, but it easily ran into the millions of dollars.

Arriving at the scene, I saw the firefighters were still actively battling the fire even though it was several hours in. They were working hard, trying to prevent damage to the surrounding buildings. I spoke briefly to a fire investigator, who advised it would be quite a while before we would be able to get close enough to the scene to begin investigating its cause.

I started by interviewing the owners and employees about the hours leading up to the fire and how it was discovered. Some of the more difficult questions required at such an emotional time were about the company's solvency and insurance coverage. I asked about maintenance and fire safety. While interviewing one person, the news coverage came on the television at the person's home and the reporter was interviewing a young man who said he had just interviewed for a job at the business. The person I was interviewing immediately said, "That's bullshit, I never seen him before." I wrote his name down as a person of interest to be interviewed as soon as possible.

I did another day of interviews and investigation as the fire scene began to cool down. I still had not had an opportunity to examine the wreckage with a fire investigator, and I knew, even if the clues were right in front of me, that I didn't have the training or expertise to know what I was seeing. I went to the staff sergeant who had assigned me the file and told him that, in view of the importance of a proper investigation, I thought I should be replaced. I knew I had done a lot of groundwork, and the police arson investigator who took the file told me he was surprised by how much I had done. I went back to patrol work, and my second date with fire ended inconclusively.

The investigation into the fire eventually ended the same way because of the total destruction of the building: "undetermined cause unknown." An important thing to note is just because police assign an arson investigator to investigate a fire, it doesn't mean the fire was an arson. They are there just in case a suspicious or unexplained fire turns out to be an arson.

In the intervening years, I still went to fires as a traffic control officer and spectator. Many of those fires were arsons. Saskatoon had a long run of arson fires, which were mostly minor, except to the victims themselves, as vehicles, fences, and garages were torched all over the city. The arsonists remained elusive and very few charges were laid.

Once I was promoted to sergeant in 2006, the role of traffic control and spectator as a constable ended abruptly. I would show up at fires and liaise with the firefighter captain or officer in charge and assign officers to assist. When the fire was suspicious, it had to be treated as a crime scene and protected until the fire investigator arrived. If the fire investigator requested a police arson investigator, it was my job to notify communications and make the request.

Unfortunately, arson investigation had become a low priority in the investigations division of the Saskatoon Police Service during the years when Saskatoon was consistently ranked in the top three cities for crime per capita in Canada. With so many issues to deal with, and new challenges emerging every year, succession planning for the trained arson investigators appeared to have fallen by the wayside. Often the officers were close to retirement and were not on call and were not obligated to be available. Sometimes it could take hours to find someone, and sometimes there was just no one available to come out. So, embarrassed and frustrated, I would tell the fire investigators that the patrol officers and I were the only help available and just take their direction until another call took us away.

One day a call came in on a day shift from a homeowner who had discovered an incendiary device attached to the natural gas inlet leading into his house. The arsonist who had planted it had ignited the fuse, but fortunately it did not cause the explosion and fire he had intended. A fire investigator and constable were at the scene with the complainant as I was rolling up on the call. Before I could get out of the car, the complainant pointed to a young man up the street and identified him as the suspect. A short chase ensued and he was in custody. He had evidence in his possession consistent with the incendiary device. Once he was secured, I turned him over to the constable to transport to the cells. I had dealt with the suspect several times over the years prior to this and he had never been involved in anything even remotely as serious as this. I told him I would be in to talk to him as soon as I was done at the scene.

There was something very off-centre with this whole incident, and I felt the whole story had yet to emerge. On the technical side it appeared to be a strong case. The failed device was not destroyed, and the evidence was fairly intact. The complainant, an older man, said he knew the suspect and had sometimes let him stay at his house over the years to help him out when he was going through tough times. As there was at least a thirty-year age difference between them, and they weren't related, I immediately became suspicious of the true nature of their relationship. He became vague on how long he knew the suspect and was sparse on details. The fire investigator felt we had a strong case for arson and said if the device had worked not only would the complainant's house have been destroyed but neighbouring houses would have been as well, with a high potential for loss of life.

Once the technical side of the investigation was done, I went in to interview the suspect. I wanted to know his motive for doing something so drastic and dangerous. He refused to talk, even though we had known each other for years. He seemed to have spent his fury and was willing to take whatever charges came his way. It was frustrating, and I was left with my suspicions but nothing else.

Around this time, a decision was made to train some patrol sergeants in level 1 arson investigation. Patrol sergeants and some constables received these courses hosted by the fire service, enabling twenty-four-hour coverage and support to fire investigations. I received the training and in short order found myself working with some very capable and knowledgeable members of the fire department.

The training of uniformed members, while a first step, was an expedient. The intent was to provide the initial support until a police investigator with a higher level of training was available. The reality was that anyone who had the level 1 course was on a list in communications, and they began getting called out when off duty to investigate fires. This was not the intention of the service. I was called several times, and while the extra pay never hurt, the call-outs for a shift worker could be very taxing. The level of exposure to toxic substances in the air after a structure fire was so high that firefighters kept a log in case a future illness could be traced to these exposures.

The police had no such policy. The smell of smoke and chemicals got into your clothes, hair, and nostrils. The firefighters helped us as much as they could by explaining and teaching us the fundamentals. The gap between our expertise and theirs remained substantial. It was, however, a good first step. I went to several house fires and a deliberate arson fire at a high school and did the initial investigations and then passed them to the arson section.

These cases finally led me to go to the inspector in charge of the criminal investigations division to talk about the state of arson investigations and the relationship between police and fire services. What troubled me was the lack of coordination and consistency between the services. It seemed to me the root cause was the scheduling of police plain clothes investigators and their availability. The lack of succession planning to replace the current investigators had unfortunately caught the police service unprepared.

The inspector told me that he was aware of these problems and had scheduled a meeting with the administration of the fire services and that steps were being taken to remedy the situation. He asked me to come to the meeting. As a result of the meeting, where everyone seemed to have checked their egos at the door, a new model of coordination emerged. More officers were trained, including younger detectives who would have several years to gain and pass on experience as they were not close to retirement. I came away with a sense of accomplishment and a feeling I had finally put the ice on the strange relationship I had with fires.

Volunteer firefighters deserve a special mention when talking about fires. They serve the communities they live in, which means they are almost always personally connected to the fires, accidents, and deaths they handle. It is something most of us never consider when we read about tragedies that occur outside of major centres with twenty-four-hour emergency coverage. These are people putting their minds and bodies at risk to protect and serve the communities they live in.

After I left policing, several tragic fires in First Nations communities in Saskatchewan sadly highlighted the importance of fire protection and firefighting. Fire protection is one of the first and foremost duties of community leaders. It cannot be scrimped on, nor can the issue be shelved for another day. When a fire occurs, it is too late to decide as leaders who was responsible for the protection of lives and property. Sometimes when leaders are trying to allocate and prioritize what a community needs, and they have not had a fire for a while, they can forget what an absolute duty it is to ensure that fire protection is in place. The size of a community does not have a bearing on the issue. However, the ability of the leaders to see the importance of this does.

CHAPTER 3
THE VALUE OF WOMEN ON POLICING'S FRONT LINE

When I was young, in the sixties and seventies, feminism was making gains in the United States and in southern Canada. Not so much, though, in my isolated home community in northern Ontario. As far as social change went, we were decades behind much of the rest of the country.

Northern communities with unique challenges did allow for some breaks from tradition for practical reasons. My Auntie Eva was an active trapper with her husband and endured the same hardships he did. Overall, though, the work force was male-dominated.

In the early seventies, I often heard the phrases "be a man," "men don't cry," and "that's women's work," which were used to shape men into what we were supposed to be. Some of this even came from my own mother as she tried to prepare us for the world.

My mother was in many ways the person who shaped my attitudes toward women in the work force. She had adopted the traditional role women were expected to fill; cooking, cleaning, and caring for the children filled her days. But, at the same time, she displayed an independence and fearlessness few of the men I knew when I was younger would dream of challenging. After my parents divorced, my mother was in a relationship with a man who beat her and tried to control her. The only good thing that came out of their relationship was my younger brother and sister. My mother survived and thrived because of how strong she was, but the contradiction between what I saw at home and what I was being told about women sat unresolved for the early part of my life.

When I first started working on the railway in 1976, to my knowledge, there was not a single woman working anywhere as part of the thousands of work crews maintaining the railway tracks across this country. There were no engineers or conductors, and I don't remember ever hearing of a woman as a train dispatcher. The railway was almost entirely male-dominated and, because I worked in isolated areas of northern Ontario, I rarely saw women and never had an opportunity to work with any of them. I had relationships and dated like everyone else, but I never worked alongside a woman. Back then, it didn't seem to be the norm anywhere.

When I joined the army and chose the combat arms, it pretty much guaranteed I would not be working with women. They were not allowed to serve in combat roles in 1978, although that has now changed. There was one female physical fitness instructor, though, when I went through basic training. Her role was clearly defined, and she was a tough instructor, but she had to be with recruits like me.

After basic training, the army dominated my next five years. I was so thoroughly indoctrinated I even had trouble relating to anyone who was not an infantryman and did not have the same values. I watched the civilian world with detached amusement and missed a lot of the eighties trends. I was working in a job where sensitivities were not even considered, and political correctness did not apply. Mission-specific and goal-orientated, the infantry in those days was like the ultimate men's club, where men were men.

My first working experience with women came when I transferred to the military police from the infantry. My unit was going to Germany, and I knew if I took the posting I would become a career infantryman and soldier. I wanted to try policing and the military police offered me a chance to be both a police officer and a soldier at the same time. As my unit had begun its rotation in Germany, and the next military police course did not start for a few months, I was transferred to the air force base in Winnipeg for on-the-job training with the military police detachment there.

The warrant officer in charge of the patrol section was welcoming and put me straight to work. Like all police services, the patrol section was made up of mostly junior members of the trade supervised by a sergeant. The biggest surprise was that our shift included one male sergeant, one male corporal, and three women—a corporal and two privates. The sergeant paired me with the male corporal, an experienced noncommissioned officer who would train me. It was all very new to me and there was a lot to learn, so I just dug in and learned as much as I could.

It turned out my education would include more than just the technicalities of the job. Inside my locker door I happened to have a pin-up picture of Tina Turner. In the photo, she was wearing a short white dress and was belting out a song. I didn't think it was offensive at all. Apparently, I was wrong. I was summoned to the warrant officer's office and told he had received a complaint. I was ordered to remove the poster.

I didn't ask who had complained. The warrant officer made it clear I was no longer in the infantry and to be more sensitive in the future.

I thought the complaint about the poster didn't represent who I was or where I had come from. I don't know why, but other men wouldn't talk down to women if I was with them, though women would tell me that some of the men I worked with were less than gracious when I wasn't around. I think my background and exposure to domestic violence at a young age reflected in my personality, and it was clear without stating it that I would not tolerate abuse of any kind.

Although there have been significant challenges along the way, the military and the police services in Canada have been leaders in implementing gender equality in a lot of ways. Being organizations where changes can be ordered and made to happen by decree, they are perfect areas for governments to experiment with social change. The military and police services in the early eighties had done away with wage discrimination; men and women earned equal pay for work of equal value. I came to realize that while changes in organizations like these could be ordered, changing attitudes would be a longer, slower, and more difficult process.

The day-to-day work on an air force base was not super busy, and it was a good place to learn the business of policing. It was also a good place to learn about working with women. I learned quickly that the women I was working with were a lot more forthcoming with their emotions and not so quick to judge people they dealt with in the course of their duties. They had challenges I hadn't even thought of, like child care and balancing their work and home lives. They had to work with some men who had little or no respect for their abilities. Some senior NCOs and officers I dealt with were definitely not with the program the military had set up for them, at least psychologically and emotionally. They worked with women as they were ordered—because they had to.

Then there were the people we were policing. Drunk servicemen could be the worst when dealing with female military police officers. They would make comments meant to hurt and sexualize the officers. Often their abusive language and behaviour simply sped up their trip to our lock-up, something I wholeheartedly approved of.

Perhaps more insidious, though, were certain men in our own military police ranks who saw these new female recruits as a liability. There were snide comments, like they'll just get pregnant, get involved in relationships with co-workers, and generally disrupt the day-to-day harmony of a male-dominated workplace. I would often retort that our male-dominated workplace could use some disruption. They would point out the differences in size and strength between men and women and how it affected their ability to do the job. I wondered about that, too, at the time, but, as you will see later on in this chapter, it was never really an issue.

There was an incident, though, after which, to my regret, I was slow to absorb the lesson it taught me about the value and wisdom of bringing women into the world of policing. I was still doing on-the-job training when my trainer and I went on a run to check some armories in the city of Winnipeg. Part of our duties was to do security checks at militia units. There were four of us on duty, plus a sergeant who occupied the guardhouse (the military police station). One military policewoman was attending the gate from inside a gatehouse. The other female officer was patrolling the base and the married quarters.

Things seemed normal that evening, until an urgent call came over the radio from my colleague at the gate. Her transmission indicated she was in serious trouble, but she offered no further details. We then tried several times to raise anyone on the radio, but nobody was answering us. The base MP should have been close, but she hadn't answered either. Both of these officers didn't have a lot of service and were still learning. Air force bases have a way of lulling military police into quiet routines of security and gate checks, and with it, perhaps, complacency. There was the odd vehicle stop or theft, but not a lot of violent calls. But this was new, and we didn't have a clue what was going on until we got there.

When we arrived, both women were in the gatehouse with the doors locked and were keeping low. They kept glancing at the guardhouse. I asked what was happening, and one of them told me the sergeant from the nearby guardhouse had tried to attack her. She had fought him off and pushed him out the door. She was very badly shaken.

From where I was, I could see the sergeant through the window, typing. Before this incident, I regarded him as a good guy, with thirty-plus years of service in the military. He was very fatherly and a good teacher. This was totally out of character for him.

I went to the door of the guardhouse and pushed it open. Something was seriously wrong. The sergeant was drooling, and he just kept hitting the same key over and over. The electric typewriter emitted a distinct tone. He didn't turn around or acknowledge me. He seemed catatonic. I slipped quietly behind him and slid his gun out of its holster and we gently escorted him to a cell. He didn't say anything. Once he was in his cell, my partner called the base security officer who was in charge of the military police section and told him what had happened. Sworn and trained military police and senior investigators came in and I was stood down.

It turned out the sergeant had suffered a nervous breakdown after his wife of thirty years had told him she was leaving. He quietly tried to deal with it on his own but couldn't and had snapped. Following his collapse, he was sent to the Department of National Defence hospital in Ottawa. Just before I left Winnipeg to go on my formal military police training he returned and I met him while on patrol. He was in civilian clothing and was doing his pre-release routine prior to leaving the military. He thanked me and apologized for what had happened.

While I was slow to appreciate it at the time, the restraint shown by the young police officer who was attacked that night at the guardhouse, and the other officer who showed up to help her, made all the difference in the outcome of this incident. Both women were armed and could have used deadly force to subdue this man, who posed a clear danger to both of them. But they wisely made the assessment to wait for backup and de-escalate a difficult and emotional situation.

As police officers, we rarely if ever expect threats from the inside, from people wearing the same uniform. It took me a while to realize the significance of this, and I am not so sure I would have shown the same restraint at that point in my service.

When I arrived at CFB Borden in Ontario, our course or serial was evenly split in numbers of men and women. To me this demonstrated the forces' commitment to gender equality and leadership. I was a proud soldier and believed each of us represented the forces in everything we did, even more so now that we were training to police our own organization. As an infantry NCO, I had high standards for dress, deportment, and physical fitness, and I expected everyone else to hold to the same. I retained my rank as master corporal until I completed the course. The military had a trade qualification system rated by completed training. As an infantryman, I was trade qualified as level six, which meant I had completed a section commander course and could lead men in the field. At completion of the military police training, I would revert to corporal at a trade level three, a trained patrol officer without supervisory rank.

Because I was an NCO, I was tasked with marching the candidates from the barracks to the Canadian Forces School of Intelligence and Security where our training took place. The candidates on the course, both men and women, had re-mustered from other trades, so they had already completed basic and trades training and were actively serving in the forces. My presumption was that they knew how to march and conduct themselves as soldiers. However, during one of the marches, one of the women kept losing step while being marched and it threw everyone off and made us look awful to anyone watching. I halted everyone and told her to get her act together in an abrupt tone. She started crying and I was at a loss. There's no crying in the army, I thought to myself. I sent her on alone and brought the rest of the course to the classroom.

I was summoned to headquarters shortly afterwards and told I was not to yell at or make anyone cry in the future. The commanding officer told me we were all learning and adapting. He dismissed my concerns about mental toughness required in the military. My attitude toward women back then wasn't improved when, during fitness training, the female candidates requested that aerobics be made a part of the course. Dancing to music I couldn't stand listening to didn't seem like army training to me. After I complained about this, my sympathetic sergeant let me lift weights or run when aerobics classes were in session.

My relationship with my female comrades took another turn for the worse when we had to take a typing class as part of the training. The minimum requirement to pass was twenty words per minute, with a 5 percent error. The corporal teaching the course was very strict about where you kept your fingers on the keyboard, and I was always reverting to the search and destroy, hunt and peck method with two fingers. One time she went to hit my hand with a ruler. I was a rank above her and it could have been an ugly incident. My accommodating sergeant once again said I could run or lift weights instead of attending typing class, as long as I could pass the typing test.

In retrospect, I don't think I was being difficult on purpose. I was learning as a man and as a leader in a totally foreign environment that I was not used to. My sergeant was ex-infantry as well; he had already made this journey and probably related to my challenges.

After this training, I was posted to an army base and there was only one female member in our section. We worked together infrequently, but I never doubted her ability to do her job. She did, however, tell me I was hard to work with. She explained I just expected everyone to keep up and didn't always take the time to explain before I acted. I had heard the same from other people before and since. It had nothing to do with gender. I just worked fast and expected the same of others.

When I started with the Saskatoon Police Service in 1987, I think there were only twelve women on the force and close to four hundred men. There were two women in our recruit class, one for Saskatoon and one for Regina. It was not long after I graduated from police college and started with the Saskatoon Police that I had a crucial insight.

I realized that women faced many of the same barriers I did as only the third Aboriginal officer on the force. You could replace racism with sexism when coming up against the long-entrenched stereotypes and consequent challenges policewomen faced in the late eighties. The women who broke the ground in the seventies told stories about having to wear skirts and high-heeled shoes and carrying their pistols in purses. They wore pillbox police caps and in many respects were treated as auxiliaries and novelties. Not all police officers were as closed-minded, but there were still some in 1987 who would sooner book off sick than work with women. My experience with the military police had helped me be a little more open-minded.

Still, though, the questions of physical ability and tough-mindedness were open for me. The women in the military had gone through a different type of training and had different experiences. A civilian woman who applied to the police may not have ever been exposed to violence, paramilitary discipline, or firearms. For my entire adult life, I'd never really been a civilian, so I had a lot to learn in order to relate to these new civilian women on the force.

More recruit classes went through after I had graduated and eventually our shift had two women. One was a university athlete and the other had a background in banking. I got to work with both of them. The other officers were relentless with their juvenile pranks aimed at us. One time someone tied a tire to, and put a "just married" sign on, the bumper of our patrol car while we were having lunch on a night shift.

The officer with the banking background was also very young. When her training officer had the day off one day, the staff sergeant told me we would be working together. By this point in my service, I was very intense and not very tolerant of inexperienced people, whether they were men or women. But I was trying to keep an open mind as we headed out onto the street.

Our first call together was a domestic dispute. A woman's ex-boyfriend had shown up at her house and damaged her car. He was still at the scene waiting for us to arrive when we rolled up. When the suspect stays at the scene after committing a crime, it's not usually remorse keeping them there. It's definitely a large red flag for police. The suspect staying at the scene usually means they believe they did nothing wrong, feel justified in their actions, or they want the confrontation with the police.

He was a big man and he was sitting on the hood of his ex-girlfriend's car with his arms crossed. My experience told me this was not going to go easy. The ex-girlfriend quickly told us enough for us to know the man had to be arrested for her safety. My partner for the day was an unknown factor. Bright and intelligent but not very big physically, I didn't know what to expect from her if this man resisted arrest, which I was sure he would. I approached the suspect, watching him clinch his jaws and shuffle to position himself to fight. I told him he was under arrest and took his elbow. He pulled away and, retaining his arm, I pulled to take him to the ground.

I'm not exactly sure what my partner did, but I think it was a classic martial arts move—using her leg to sweep the feet of the suspect out from under him. The suspect and I had not even reached the ground before she had his free arm under control. We quickly had him handcuffed and he was in custody. I'm not sure who was more surprised, the suspect or me. I looked at the officer and smiled. Afterwards I felt guilty, though, about having any doubts as to her ability to engage with a resisting suspect. For me, a lifetime of mixed messages about women and their abilities was unravelling. The two female constables on our shift were outstanding police officers, and I trusted them with my life on more than one occasion.

Just as I was making personal progress in gender relations, there came a time period when police hiring slowed down for almost ten years. Very few officers were behind me in seniority for the longest time due to the economy and Saskatchewan's slow growth. Consequently, not a lot of police officers of any gender were hired during that period of time. The women who were there then were sometimes given cases simply because they were women. Sexual assaults were often handed off to women because the investigators would assume female victims would be more forthcoming with female officers. From my experience, this was not true in most cases and, from where I was sitting, I think the assumption was more for the investigators' convenience than anything else.

The changing of attitudes is like so many things in a loop or cycle that has to be repeated periodically. Each new generation of police officers learns the lessons the preceding generation has learned but hopefully quicker, so the loop or cycle is shorter.

During the years the Saskatoon Police was involved in controversy and under scrutiny over allegations of mistreatment of First Nations people, a lot of senior officers chose to retire. This meant there was a large influx of young officers, and many were women. I was slow to notice the changes as I was so caught up in the day-to-day operations as a patrolman. I had made up my mind years ago I would work with anyone as long as they were capable. I thought most of my generation and the younger male officers felt the same, until I was promoted to sergeant.

After I was promoted, I was assigned as a patrol sergeant in the central division of Saskatoon, where I had worked most of my career. During the period of growth in the Saskatoon Police Service, many of the senior officers had competed for and attained positions in the investigative sections, leaving patrol with very junior members. I came to a shift with an almost 40/60 ratio of women to men. My team was split fifty-fifty.

The crime rate was extremely high, and we were very busy. I was excited to work with such an eclectic group of people. There were the usual issues of personality clashes and differing work ethics that any supervisor deals with. I didn't think gender was an issue for anyone.

One day there was an armed robbery on a day shift, and the suspect was on the run near a local campus. I was heading there to assist when I heard one of my favourite phrases over the air: "Suspect in custody." I got to the scene just as the prisoner was being transported to detention to get an update and make sure we had everything covered evidence-wise.

When I got there, two of the female officers at the scene looked mad. I asked what was wrong and, in language that would have made a trucker blush, one of them told me the male officers had cut her off and made the arrest. She said it happened a lot on serious calls. I was taken aback and wondered if it was just sour grapes until the other officer confirmed it in a calmer manner. I listened but did not make any commitment or comment. I wanted to think this situation out.

Ego, as I have said many times before, can be a police officer's worst enemy, and from experience I knew police officers are highly competitive by nature. This was different because it was a gender issue. Were the male officers unconsciously taking on the role of protector, or did they see themselves as more capable than the women? I wanted a smoothly functioning team and having to deal with something like this made me angry. Because there was so much crime and so many junior members, I couldn't afford to alienate anyone. And simply ordering the men on my team to be more reasonable about their female colleagues probably wasn't going to get me very far.

I decided to take another approach. I began taking the female officers with me everywhere I went where there might be trouble. We went to drug houses, addresses of suspects wanted on outstanding warrants, and to make arrests when suspects had been identified after a crime. In short order, the women were leading in the statistics for arrests, and for drugs and weapons seizures. We had some outstanding arrests and more than a few physical altercations. After a month or two, one of the male officers came into my office as a spokesperson for the other men and told me there was a feeling on the shift that I was favouring the female officers. I acknowledged his message and said I would take it under consideration. What I was actually thinking was *how does that feel?* But I never said it out loud.

I think the message got through and everyone started working better as a team. I was learning by teaching as well. As a supervisor working with women over that period and in the years afterwards, I came to appreciate immensely the different strengths both women and men brought to policing.

Sadly, since I retired, the two largest organizations that were mandated to push for equality between genders have both come under scrutiny for the way female soldiers and police officers have been treated within their organizations. The Canadian Armed Forces and the Royal Canadian Mounted Police were publicly forced to acknowledge sexual abuse and sexism against female members by male officers. For years the military and police were leaders in creating representative forces. It's obvious some police officers and soldiers still see women as exploitable and not equal. In my opinion, these officers shouldn't be wearing the uniform. Like racists, they will be weeded out eventually. Women in the services need to report harassment and outlast the sexists for change to occur.

As a citizen now, I think as disturbing as the stories are about abuse and harassment, I am optimistic the openness will help change attitudes. I know it's no consolation to the women who had to endure the small-mindedness of the perpetrators. I am sure I don't know the half of what they went through. They are brave women to come forward and act as leaders for the women who will follow them.

I was, in every respect, a hard-assed street cop for many years. I grew up in a culture where toughness was admired in soldiering and policing. But I learned from and was changed by the women I worked with. My take-away was women were more inclined to diffuse confrontations via communication. Women were less inclined to escalate situations when someone challenged their authority, but it didn't mean they would shy away from using force if they had to. Those skills become more and more important as police are being increasingly scrutinized with each passing year.

Having a police service representative of the community it serves is ultimately what every community should be striving for. It only makes sense to have as many women as you can in a police service. There is still a bit of work to do.

In March 2016 I took part in an initiative with Roz Kelsey and the University of Regina to create a YouTube video called "Man Up Against Violence: Redefining What It Means to Man Up." It was supposed to focus on helping to reduce or prevent violence against women. An unexpected bonus was the way the men who talked on the video expressed, whether they realized it or not when they were saying it, that changing attitudes was a starting point for a new, respectful, and long overdue fairness in our society.

Do I get it right every time? Hell, no! I can use all the help I can get from like-minded people. If you've seen it and experienced it in a field like policing, you will know the value of equality. I know I do.

CHAPTER 4
BRINKSMANSHIP—
THE USE OF FORCE, PART 1

During my separate but related careers in the military and the police, I was given a solemn and awesome responsibility. As both a cop and a soldier, I was among the relatively small number of people in Canadian society legally allowed to use force against my fellow human beings—deadly force if necessary. I suppose I understood that from my very first days in uniform, but I didn't fully comprehend the reality of actually holding someone's life in my hands until my days as a young soldier peacekeeping in Cyprus.

I did my six-month tour of duty in Cyprus in the fall and spring of 1982 and 1983. My unit was the 2nd Battalion of the Princess Patricia's Canadian Light Infantry Regiment, and I was a detachment commander with the reconnaissance platoon. Elements of our unit, including the reconnaissance platoon, were posted to Ledra Palace Hotel, a former five-star hotel in the middle of the city of Nicosia. It was once a grand hotel. President John F. Kennedy had apparently stayed there during a state visit many years before the conflict that had divided the island. During the fighting, the hotel had taken some damage from gunfire and shrapnel. The scars were on the outside and inside walls to remind us of why we were there.

In the years since the fighting and the hotel's seizure by Canadian forces, the building had deteriorated, as only essential repairs were allowed in order to keep the place running. Some windows and entrances had been sandbagged and the sandbags covered in heavy plastic. It is weird, thinking back on it now, how the coils of razor wire didn't seem out of place—it was all just part of the landscape. Still, the palace was a solid building, with a ballroom and lounges converted into mess halls and less than glamorous military assignments. The entrance and lobby were spacious and had the feel of a grand hotel from the fifties.

Long gone were the glory days of Ledra Palace. I wondered what the owners of the hotel thought of the thousands of young soldiers who occupied their building during the long tenure of Canada's mission there. The Greek Cypriots, the Turkish Cypriots, and other representatives with a stake in the island still held regular meetings, trying to come to some sort of agreement on how to reunite their homeland during my tour there. Sadly, the impasse that caused the war and Turkish invasion is still unresolved. The island remains split to this day.

One day we were called to the reconnaissance platoon headquarters building and briefed by our captain on an operation called "Locksmith." During this operation we were to provide security to delegates from both sides who were meeting in one of the conference rooms of the palace. I don't think the delegates were very high-ranking because everyone seemed pretty relaxed about Locksmith. My detachment was assigned to part of the roof of Ledra Palace to provide overwatch. There were no specific rules of engagement other than the anemic United Nations rules. The UN required verbal challenges before engaging, which were not practical at the best of times, much less from a roof of a hotel. There were no threat assessments, or if there were they weren't shared with the soldiers who might encounter them. None of the detailed planning I would have expected was forthcoming, so, as all soldiers do, we improvised.

The area I was in charge of overlooked the Turkish checkpoint closest to the conference room chosen for the meeting. It was not a good position. The height of the palace and the range to the targets, if there were any, would have made us fairly ineffective. As well, having a high vantage point lets you see an area well—it also makes you a highly visible target. Still, for my detachment and me, it was exciting to be part of something different from patrols and possibly important. Cyprus is a beautiful island, with enormous potential because of its strategic location. If only the Greeks and Turks could settle their issues.

I took my position on post, lying on some sandbags and scanning the area with binoculars, looking for anything unusual. After an hour or so, the initial excitement was gone, and we settled in under the hot sun, hoping the diplomats would wrap it up quickly. A fuel truck drove up to the Turkish checkpoint and stopped. The truck was directly opposite the conference room hosting the diplomats. The driver, whoever he was, had my full attention. I propped myself up and put my rifle sights on the driver's side door of the truck. My heart was pounding. I breathed in and out slowly to calm and steady myself.

A million thoughts were racing through my mind. Who was this driver and what was he doing stopping at that spot? Should I sound the alarm? Were my guys and I going to survive a fuel truck explosion if this was a terrorist attack? The door to the truck opened and the driver casually got out. I sighted in on him and rested my trigger finger on the trigger guard. He was oblivious to me as he walked to the base of a tree and opened his lunch bag. He probably had no idea there was a diplomatic meeting taking place a few metres from his choice of a lunch spot.

The few seconds this incident took to unfold left a deep impression on me and stuck with me for years afterwards. I stayed on high alert until the driver got back in his truck and drove away after his lunch. I stayed keyed up until the operation was stood down. The lack of a thorough briefing on what the situation was and what the threat levels were left the reaction to the fuel truck as a potential bomb totally to my own discretion. If I had overreacted, I could have started or restarted a conflict. If I had underestimated the situation, I could have allowed a terrorist attack to occur with the same results. The trucker never knew it, but lives were at stake in this incident. Fortunately, I didn't have to take his life or risk losing mine.

Threat assessments and thorough briefings can help with decision making in crisis situations. Experience hopefully fills in the gaps. Determining whether the use of force was necessary and appropriate was something I was confronted with many times in my career as a police officer. When to act or react are decisions thousands of police officers make across Canada every day. Like a carefully orchestrated diplomatic dance, I called this part of policing brinksmanship. Brinksmanship takes place during the very few initial seconds in every conflict or encounter where a decision has to be made as to whether or not to use force. We have all seen the consequences of the rapid decisions of police to use force when it was later deemed unnecessary or excessive by the court of public opinion or by the actual courts if charges were laid. What we rarely see or hear about is when the decision to use force was the right one or the only one available, and it saved lives.

During my first year of policing with the military police, I served in Wainwright, Alberta. CFB Wainwright was and still is a major Canadian Forces training base. It is the permanent home to the Princess Patricia's Canadian Light Infantry Battle School and had, at that time, about 1,200 permanent staff. It also has a huge training area with the capacity to host thousands of soldiers holding major exercises. British, American, and Canadian soldiers descend, budgets permitting, on Wainwright annually to practise the art of war. When there was a major exercise, our twelve-man detachment was supplemented by the military police officers attached to the units deployed on the exercise.

Military police officers who are attached to combat units have a variety of roles they must master that are exclusive to them, however, not all the military police officers deployed to a field exercise are assigned to reinforce the garrison military police. They remain in the field, learning the tasks they will have to perform in the event of a war. The handling of prisoners of war, large unit traffic control, and guarding headquarters units are among just a few of their responsibilities. As a result, those units could only spare a few officers to help the Wainwright garrison military police control the thousands of soldiers who were given breaks in training to go to the town of Wainwright to blow off a little steam and have a few beers. As you can imagine, even the release of just five hundred soldiers for a few hours with access to alcohol can turn a town with a 1985 population of five thousand people into a challenging policing problem.

I used to be one of those soldiers, though often I would just stay in the field rather than go into town because I knew there would be fighting and other alcohol-related issues. So when the exercise started, I knew we would be busy. Even early in my career as a police officer, I knew making highly visible patrols in a marked patrol car in uniform was a useful deterrent to would-be troublemakers. The more sensible people would sound the alarm to those who were starting to get rowdy, and sometimes that was all it took to keep people in line. I started a night shift on a beautiful summer evening and, after doing a patrol of the base, I headed downtown to fly the flag.

I drove to downtown Wainwright, which was, in 1985, just a long main street like so many other small Canadian towns. I drove the entire length of the main drag up until the highway and turned around to make another pass before heading back to base. There were quite a few soldiers in town at the bars, restaurants, and pizza parlours, all in uniform and seemingly well-behaved. Because the soldiers were on exercise, they all wore combat uniforms. The general rule was when you were in uniform, and in the public eye, you had to wear your beret and conduct yourself in a manner that did not bring disrespect to the forces. The military police were there to enforce those rules. On duty that night, policing the town and area of Wainwright in addition to myself, were two American military police officers, one British military police officer, and two Royal Canadian Mounted Police officers. On the base and in the training, there were approximately fifteen thousand American, British, and Canadian soldiers. The exercise was scheduled for six weeks.

On my way back downtown, I saw a solitary soldier, which in and of itself was unusual because the troops moved in groups, walking without headdress. For Canadian combat troops out of the field, the beret was the standard issue, and you were supposed to wear it when you were not in a building. I pulled up beside him. He ignored me, which I quickly learned was one of the most significant signs of impending violence in police and suspected offender contacts. The average person without disabilities notices when a police car pulls up alongside of them. There is almost always a reaction. If a person has done nothing wrong, they might be offended or curious. If they have done something wrong, they will run or try to talk their way out of their situation. Very rarely does a person completely ignore the presence of the police. This soldier just kept trucking along.

I got out of the patrol car and he just kept walking. I had to trot to catch up to him, and when I caught up and got in front of him he just tried to walk past me. I announced I was military police and told him to put on his beret then catch up with his guys and call it a night. He brushed past me. This was an affront to everything I was trying to do. I touched his forearm and asked for his CAFIB.20 (Canadian Forces Identification Card) and he pushed past me. I reached out and touched his forearm again and told him he was under arrest and, after that, the fight was on.

He didn't try to escape or run. He turned toward me and adopted a fighting stance. He was a little unsteady on his feet and seemed to be having trouble focusing. He smelled strongly of alcohol. What got me was he wasn't saying anything—no curses or pleas to be left alone. He was intent on fighting me for whatever reason, and there didn't appear to be anything deterring him from what was about to happen. I wasn't going to engage in a fist fight on the street in the middle of Wainwright, Alberta. I thought he was intoxicated enough that a quick side-step and tackle would allow me to get him in handcuffs. I made a quick radio call to the other military police to alert them to my situation and made my move.

He wasn't as drunk as he first appeared and was obviously skilled. I got a hold of him for a second and he countermoved, dropping his hips and slipping out of my grip. He threw a high kick at my head, narrowly missing me. He was wearing combat boots, and if he had connected I would have been hurt. I was too inexperienced to realize my best course of action would have been to disengage and wait for backup. I quickly came to the conclusion that all of my military police unarmed combat and control training was going to be tested by this soldier. We did not carry batons, chemical agents, or electronic stun guns back then, so I had no way to even the odds against a stronger and well-trained arrest other than to shoot him.

We were right beside a bank, and I knew my best chance of successfully getting this man into handcuffs would be if I could close the distance between us and get him in a chokehold. Closing the distance and using the wall of the building prevented him from throwing those devastating kicks at me. He was getting better and more focused with each of my takedown attempts and he still hadn't said a word. We had been on the ground several times by this point, and we were both picking up minor injuries. Anyone who has ever been in a fight can tell you a minute seems like an eternity. We had been engaged for several minutes before two American military police officers rolled up in a Jeep.

I was so totally focused on this soldier that I couldn't have told you if there was anyone watching or if there were any other threats other than him. I had tunnel vision. A phenomenon, I would learn as my career progressed, that was not uncommon in a high-stress situation but one that can get you killed or injured when you are a street cop. Sometimes you get so focused on what you are doing you forget to check the environment around you. His comrades could have showed up, or a sympathetic like-minded person who hated the police could have happened upon us and turned the tables in his favour.

Once the American military police officers showed up, I thought he might surrender and let himself be taken into custody. They grow American military police big. I was close to being gassed when they arrived. Gassed, for you nonfighters, means I was tired and doubting my ability to take this guy into custody. I was losing. The two American MPs were great guys.

One was a star pitcher in college, and the other one wanted to be a civilian cop in Huntington Beach, California, when he left the army. I got my third wind and the three of us rushed this soldier. He fought back with a renewed vigour, as if increasing the odds against him reinvigorated him.

He broke free of control holds and gang tackles. He seemed to have no pain threshold whatsoever. The main concern by now was getting this soldier into custody without hurting him. A British military police officer and a member of the Wainwright RCMP detachment showed up. The RCMP member had been alerted to the struggle by citizens concerned with the early evening brawl taking place on their main street. Between the five of us we managed to isolate every limb and get him into handcuffs. He still had not said a word.

Both the arrested soldier and I were bloodied up with scrapes and minor cuts. My uniform was a mess and I was tired. The American military police officers said they would follow me up to the guardhouse in case round two started while I was booking him in. When we arrived, he followed all instructions as I searched him and inventoried his property. He was released from his handcuffs at his cell door. He only nodded his head yes or no in response to questions. When he was in his cell, he just sat down on his haunches, seemingly no worse for wear. I found his identification card and contacted his unit.

When I talked to a senior NCO and informed him I had a member of his unit in custody, he immediately asked if any police officers had been injured. When I told him I'd experienced minor scrapes while making the arrest, he expressed surprise and relief. He told us the soldier we had arrested had been an unarmed combat instructor in the airborne regiment. Fortunately, this particular paratrooper was having an off-day, which prevented me from having an even worse one.

As I learned that day, as an MP and again later as a civilian officer, the use of force by police is almost always ugly. No matter how professional, no matter how much an officer's use of force is in adherence with the law and policy, it always looks ugly.

I have seen and been a part of many violent arrests. Suspects in these cases may have been intent on assaulting, robbing, or even killing before my colleagues and I caught up to them. Then they may have tried resisting arrest and escaping. If they had learned that avoiding arrest wasn't going to work and they had an audience of bystanders, or even other criminals, they would often try to turn the tables on the police. They would scream that they were being hurt or that they were not resisting as the police stopped and overpowered them. This almost always struck a chord with onlookers, regardless of their background. I understand the sentiment, because the natural inclination of most people is to favour the underdog in conflict with the larger power of the state. As often as I could, I would try to explain the circumstances of a violent arrest to onlookers once the situation was under control. However, sometimes it was just not possible, so the only conclusions the witnesses could come to were based on their own personal values or bias. Criminals, from my experiences, are always ready to exploit this reaction from the public at large.

Excessive or unjustified use of force is the most scrutinized of police and civilian interactions and can undo years of good relations with a community. Over the course of my career, the prevention of excessive or unjustified use of force was always a leadership and training issue. There was an institutional culture element as well if a police service allowed or practised hard arrest techniques or didn't update training on a regular basis. It became a cultural norm and a continued practice for new officers. Over the years, some criminals told me they avoided some cities because "the cops always roughed you up." It may have just been criminal bravado, but, if true, these cities served as good examples of a police service institutional culture left unchecked.

Here was where the front lines were for me and thousands of young police officers in the late 1980s. I made it known very early on in my career that I was not a fan of cheap shots, or the extra strike after an arrest was in custody. The officers I worked with picked up on this very quickly. Like-minded officers made their impact on interactions between suspects and police as well. Policing was changing and so were society's expectations of the police. I don't fault the generations of police officers that came before me, some of whom dealt with criminals harshly. It was what worked for them—and what old-time criminals expected. Many people have told me over the years that they wished the police could still give young offenders a good swift kick in the ass, or a cuff in a foul mouth, and then never see a courtroom.

The realities have changed and that is just the way life goes. People have rights, and their rights circumvent police short-cuts or the human tendency to be lazy. The days when a police report would read "a struggle ensued, and the arrest was sub-dued" or "the subject violently resisted arrest; the subject was overpowered and taken into custody" have long faded into police folklore. Saskatoon police officers—and I would hope every police officer across Canada—have to justify, document, and detail why and how force was used when making an arrest.

I have used force many times, either acting or reacting over the course of my career. From the start of my career right up to my very last night on the streets, I made decisions that affected people and could be judged. Deciding when to act or react was a fact of life for me and continues to be for every officer still serving in Canada.

Did I get it right every time? The answer to the question is simply...no. It would be impossible to get it right every time. There are just too many variables in violent and fluid situations. I have already written about shoot or don't shoot situations in my first two books. Unforeseen factors that affect the outcome of using force when making an arrest can and have changed both police officers' and suspects' lives. I was very lucky no one ever died or was critically injured over the course of my career when I had to use force, and I know it. This is a complex area, though, loaded with dilemmas, and I'm going to have more to say about it later on in this book.

CHAPTER 5
MAKING POLICE

I finished my last patrol with the military police in Wainwright, Alberta, on a Sunday, and, after turning my gear in, I headed to the Saskatchewan Police College to start classes on Monday. My roommate, an RCMP officer, graciously drove me to Regina. I didn't have much with me: a barrack box, some civilian clothes, a radio, and my uniforms and equipment from the Saskatoon Police. It was pretty much everything I owned. When my room-mate left to go back to Wainwright, I realized he was the last person I knew, and I was now truly on my own. When I arrived at the police college, I was two weeks late. When you put in your release request from the military, you are required to stay in the forces for six months from the date your release is approved. The military had tried to invoke a rarely used clause in the National Defence Act, where it could keep a serving soldier who had requested release in order to maintain the manpower of an essential trade. After a bit of wrangling and nail-biting, we finally worked out an agreement to let me use the remaining leave I was entitled to so I could make the six-month window. I was the first candidate in Saskatchewan Police College history to be allowed to start two weeks late. I was actually on leave from the Canadian Forces for about a month when I started working for the City of Saskatoon.

My experiences with the military helped me get a job with the Saskatoon Police. Being a qualified Indigenous candidate didn't hurt either. Very few Indigenous people were applying to municipal police departments in 1987. The majority of candidates looking for a job applied to the RCMP, who were actively recruiting from First Nations communities.

The Saskatchewan Police College is located on, and is part of, the University of Regina campus. All municipal police in Saskatchewan train there, while the RCMP, being a national police force, has its own training depot also located in Regina. The police recruits in 1987 lived in the part of the university called College West in the dormitories with the other students. Everyone had individual rooms, except me and the poor guy who had a room to himself until I got there. The police recruits were in eight room dorms, with a common area and a small kitchen. The campus and university life were pretty foreign to me. I had taken one course at the University of Manitoba when I was with the military police, but it was an evening class. I didn't know anyone in Regina or, for that matter, anyone in Saskatchewan. With the University of Regina's emphasis on academic freedom and freedom of expression, being a police recruit was like being the ultimate outsider on campus.

My fellow recruits were for the most part from Saskatchewan or Alberta and had many different backgrounds, though none were ex-military. They had already formed friendships in the two weeks prior to my arriving. I just tried to fit in the best I could. The idea of putting a provincial police college on a university campus seemed odd to me. Most of the other recruits had university or college degrees, so the campus was a familiar place for them.

As an army guy, it went against what I had experienced in the military. Military training facilities were almost always far removed from civilians. Military police training was my first experience with co-ed training, but it took place on a security-controlled Canadian Forces base with minimal interaction with civilians. I was only on the Regina campus for a couple of weeks when a young man from another campus flashed a butterfly knife at me. A butterfly knife is like a switchblade and is a prohibited weapon in Canada. He was a Native fellow and was testing me. I told him the knife would bring more trouble than it was worth and to get rid of it. I was not yet a police officer in Saskatchewan, so I didn't act on the offence. It irked me because a month earlier, as a military policeman, I would have disarmed and arrested him.

All the other recruits, except one or two from Alberta, would go home on the weekends. I didn't have anywhere to go, so I stayed on the campus. I did a lot of running and exploring Regina. I stopped keeping a mileage log after six hundred–plus kilometres. Police training at the Saskatchewan Police College was pretty straightforward. We learned criminal law, report writing, firearms, and defensive tactics. We learned a host of provincial statutes, general knowledge, and crisis intervention techniques. Canadian police are well trained compared to some other countries. Police services are constantly improving and increasing training to meet new expectations. We did a fair amount of scenario training, which, after my experiences in the military police, seemed awkward and unrealistic. I had already learned in the military that the best-laid plans never survive initial contact.

The psychical training was good, provided by instructors who were serving police officers from Saskatchewan who were seconded to the college. Police officers with real-life experiences and practical knowledge were the best kind of instructors to have. They had a vested interest in turning out good competent police officers. I cannot speak for the rest of the country, but in Saskatchewan the main difference between police training and other corporations' training schemes is the screening of the candidates prior to attending training.

In 1987—and to this day—it is exceptionally hard to get hired as a police officer. When I applied to the Saskatoon Police in 1987, there were a thousand applicants for twelve positions. The initial written test and application forms remove many people from the process in the early stages. The physical abilities test has changed over the years as well. When I applied, the abilities test was a timed run, pull-ups, sit-ups, push-ups, and obstacles. Now it's a standardized test called a POPAT (Police Officer Physical Abilities Test). It is a timed series of challenges that represents all the aspects of the physical activity a police officer may face in under five minutes. A large number of potential candidates surprisingly wash out at the physical testing stage. After passing the POPAT, an applicant's references are contacted, and background checks are conducted, as the applicant advances through the hiring process—more than a few people are eliminated as a result.

Since I was hired, more levels of testing have been added. The candidates have to take a psychological test and submit to a polygraph examination. All of these steps take place before a highly stressful final interview. Of course, an applicant's education, community involvement, and history of volunteerism all factor into the decision to hire a police officer. My advice to any young person wanting to be a police officer is to know the standards and train to meet or exceed them. Be determined and stay off social media if you aren't absolutely committed to what you share as a reflection of you and your values. The standard advice of "don't do drugs" and "stay away from bad influences" is always there.

But no system is perfect, and some people get through all the screening only to fail at police college. Several things can end a candidate's career before they get going. Not maintaining fitness levels after testing and prior to college can lead to a downfall. Deceit or deception with fellow candidates, instructors, or the public will have you turning in your gear and get you on the first bus out of Regina in a heartbeat. Rarely, the inability to master a firearm or driving skills will end a potential police officer's career. Administrations and some leaders look on failures at police college as failures in the system.

I take the opposite tack. I believe officers who fail to meet the standards required in the early stages, when the stakes are personal, will be problem officers in the future. Better to have them fail early on than put the public or the service employing them at risk. Unfortunately, some people tie a lot of their self-worth to their dream of becoming a police officer. In my experience, once they come to realize it's not going to happen, they successfully get on with their lives.

After graduating from police training, recruits are still not in the clear. A period of field training follows and, depending on the agency, it can vary from six months to a year. The officer is paired up with a field trainer. The FTO (field training officer) will teach the everyday practical aspects of policing to the officer. How to interact with people, officer safety, and reporting are just a few of the thousands of things a rookie needs to know. All the while, the FTO submits updates and progress reports as the officer's skills develop. Some officers never make it out of this training. While they may have made out well in the controlled environment at police college, they may lack the skills to successfully work in real-life situations and they are let go. Whether the average citizen thinks about it or not, the "stupid cop" who took their report or gave them a ticket has been well tested and trained by the time they encounter them.

Learning to be a civilian police officer didn't come without surprises. In the military we called civilians "civies" and watched them with a sense of amused detachment. Now I was living and training on a campus full of them. I was in about the tenth week of training, and I walked into the cafeteria in uniform to get something eat. I didn't realize it at the time, but I was about to get a lesson in democracy, one that pushed me out of my comfort zone that, up until then, had involved living inside the military and then in a paramilitary situation as a civilian police recruit. An Indigenous man was seated at a table, and on the wall behind him was a Canadian flag hung upside down. He was wearing a black beret (in my old world, only armoured soldier units wore black berets).

He was protesting something, and I was instantly angry. The flag stood for something to me. It stood for respect, honour, and duty. The flag represented this great country we lived in. Freedom and all the privileges of being Canadian were being disrespected, I thought. The beret, not properly earned, was the next thing. Soldiers earn the right to wear the berets through effort, training, and determination. *Who was this guy?* To top it off, a CBC reporter, also Indigenous, and her camera operator turned up to interview him. I got my lunch and went off, wondering if I should have just stayed in the army.

Afterwards, though, I did some thinking. A protester who pushed every button there was to push for a recently released ex-soldier made me realize one of the reasons I had signed up in the first place was to protect his right to protest, whether I agreed with him or not. It was also my first real-life encounter with a CBC reporter (or, for that matter, any kind of reporter). She was just doing her job.

Besides, I'd always loved the CBC because it was often the only radio station we could listen to in northern Ontario in the daytime and early evening hours. I grew up listening to *As It Happens* and a host of other CBC radio shows. The newscasts made me feel worldly. The few times I did watch television growing up, it was *The Beachcombers* and, my favourite, *Front Page Challenge*.

Upon further reflection, I came to appreciate that the protestor, the reporter, and I were all Indigenous people in our twenties, all trying to make changes in the world in the same place at the same time. I had never been in a situation like that before. All of us were trying to be leaders in our own way. The whole encounter was a big deal to me in 1987.

I carried on with training and was getting close to graduation. I still didn't have a place to live in Saskatoon and it was coming down to the wire. I came to see the reasoning of putting police recruits on a university campus. At first, I thought it was an experiment in liberalism and poorly thought out. I now saw the benefits of putting police recruits where they were in the public eye at all times. In my opinion, it made for better police officers when police recruits had to conduct themselves in a professional manner whenever they weren't in their classrooms or quarters. Learning how to be a civilian police officer wasn't without its surprises, and I'm sure I wasn't as open-minded as I thought I was. Still, I was getting there.

Our police class had been one of the largest in many years, with candidates from the Regina, Prince Albert, Saskatoon, Weyburn, and Cudworth police departments. After we graduated and all the officers went to their respective departments, I lost touch with these peers. It's the nature of municipal policing that, unless you are part of a joint task force or in the specialty investigative sections, you rarely see members from other departments except for training courses at the college.

Of the twelve other officers hired by the City of Saskatoon, we were distributed between the four watches or platoons of uniformed officers, providing twenty-four-hour patrol coverage to the city. You lose track of the members who go to opposite shifts and, unless there are social events, you rarely see them. They go on with their careers, and you go on with yours. Of all my classmates, twenty-nine years later, only four are still working. All are senior NCOs, staff sergeants, or sergeants in patrol or investigative sections. Five retired early, either as a result of injuries or to pursue other employment. The other three retired after I did. Most of them did investigative work at some point in their careers, from criminal intelligence to homicide investigations. Two were outstanding K9 officers with enough stories to write books, I am sure.

I had some unique challenges after graduation and deployment onto the streets of Saskatoon as a police officer. I didn't know the city at all. I didn't know the streets or the infrastructure. I didn't know a single person other than my fellow classmates from the college. In some ways this was good because I would never be put in the position of arresting a friend or relative, which can happen if you police in the city you grew up in.

I found a furnished basement apartment at the last minute, a couple of blocks from the police station, just before graduation. There were a lot of other things I hadn't thought of when I made the switch from the military to civilian policing. I had to get a phone and all the other things I had taken for granted or was provided with over the years. I bought a map of the city and rented a car to try to learn the streets. I rode the bus and walked a lot in the downtown.

Still, there were times during my field training when I didn't have a clue where I was or where I was going in Saskatoon. In one incident, a short pursuit started with an erratic driver, and my FTO, who was at the wheel of our cruiser, told me to call it in, that is radio in our location and the direction of our pursuit. Trying to read street signs at speeds approaching 100 kilometres an hour at night isn't an easy task at the best of times—in other words, I was seriously disoriented.

With experience, though, I did get my bearings and was able to do the job to the best of my abilities, as do fifty thousand officers serving in Canada every day. And that's all due to the good training I received in police college and from my mentors who trained me from my first days on the street. Training and experience give us the police we see.

CHAPTER 6
WHAT WOULD YOU TELL A YOUNG CONSTABLE?

I've been asked many times since I retired what I would tell a prospective police recruit or a young constable just starting their career, as I was in the late '80s. Now that I've left policing, I answer, "Well, actually…"

When I was a working police officer, including my time as a sergeant, I was never once asked to teach at the Saskatchewan Police College. However, after I retired, I have spoken to every recruit class since. I feel honoured and grateful for being given the privilege to speak to recruits in their first month of training. The quality and intelligence of these officers never ceases to amaze me. The messages I try to convey are all from hard-earned experience. I cover a fair bit of ground in the two hours I get them for. One of the many things I talk about is the necessity of getting to know your community—all of it. For any police officer, in any jurisdiction, getting to know the community you work in should be one of your primary missions. Being as familiar as you can be with the people and area you police will help you every day you are on the streets.

Especially important is getting to know the people who will take up the majority of your time in your area. These are the "invisible people," the term I use for the people who most of the community ignores unless they are unable to. The alcoholics, drug addicts, and mentally ill people in the area you police will take a disproportionate amount of your time on the street. If you get to know their backstories, you will inevitably build a relationship at some level.

These relationships can last your entire career. They also give officers valuable insight and perspective as to how and why these people became who they are. I have given examples in my first two books but, even with knowing the importance of getting to know people, it's easy to forget how important it is as you go about your duties. I remember one fellow who really helped to cement how important knowing the backstory is.

There was a particularly nasty and mean-spirited alcoholic who aggressively panhandled and drank anything he could get his hands on. He was a couple of years younger than me. He had a loving family and a caring support network. In spite of this, he still went on binges, and his erratic behaviour and mean-spiritedness constantly brought him into contact with the police.

His older brothers were also alcoholics but with none of the hatred this man regularly displayed. He had a special dislike for me, "the fucking apple cop," "the white man's Indian," and he pushed all the right buttons whenever I had to deal with him. One day, after I had been promoted to sergeant, I was telling one of the younger constables about him to prepare her, since she would inevitably have to deal with him at some point. She told me she had already had an encounter with him and that he had told her his mother had been shot to death, murdered in front of him at a young age. His brothers hadn't witnessed the crime but had lost their mother as well.

I don't know why this man told the young constable this. Maybe it was her nonconfrontational demeanour or because he was feeling the need to explain himself to someone. It was a very poignant moment for me, and I saw this man in a whole new light. He remained mean-spirited toward everyone, and especially toward me when he was drinking. I knew in my heart it wasn't personal and that it was the direct result of unresolved trauma. Some people find ways past trauma and pain. He could not, and I still arrested him when I had to. Knowing the backstories of otherwise invisible people is huge and will only benefit you as a police officer and the citizens you serve.

The next group of people I tell recruits they need to learn about once they are on the streets are what I call the "highly visible and dangerous people." These are the active criminals, predators, drug dealers, gang members, and violent abusers. New ones emerge constantly, but most of the highly visible and dangerous have long been working on their criminal résumés. Their very existence—if officers are honest with themselves—is part of the reason why a lot of police sign up in the first place: to stop and catch the bad guys. I say bad *guys* because the over-whelming majority of criminals are male. More women are getting involved in gangs and crime, but they are still vastly outnumbered by male offenders. Technology has now made getting to know your active criminals a little easier than when I first started with the Saskatoon Police. When I first started, computer systems were just coming online, and often the only way to read reports was to pull hard copies out of cen-tral records. Photos of criminals were classified by local record numbers, and you actually had to pull their pictures from boxes filed numerically by their local record numbers. It was a lot of work and time-consuming when you were supposed to be on the streets patrolling. Now new officers can access data banks and photographs from their in-car computers in seconds when looking for information.

Nothing can replace actual face-to-face contact with the criminally active people in the community you are policing. They learn what you are about and you learn what they are about. The equivalent in the sports world is watching game tapes to learn the other team's plays. To recognize an active criminal on sight and to be recognized as an officer capable of knowing criminals on sight is a very powerful enforcement tool. Knowing that the police know you is also a strong deterrent for many criminals. Learn, remember, and expect adaptation to your abilities as your skill increases, because active criminals are responsible for a lot of the misery and crime in the area you will be assigned or choose.

Police officers also have to build relationships with the people who are active criminals. You have to learn their stories. Learning their stories will give an officer insight and sometimes help avoid a violent arrest or confrontation. For example, one cocaine dealer known for his violent tendencies and explosive temper mellowed once I discovered he was dyslexic. I told him not to take his frustrations with his dyslexia out on people and he actually listened. He still dealt cocaine and I still arrested him when I had to, but there was a modem of understanding between us.

The reason why I emphasize these groups to recruits is because, for most people who have lived a life free of contacts with addicts, the mentally ill, and criminals, this life is entirely new ground. The standards for hiring police officers sometimes can exclude applicants who have had life experience with these groups. Questionable associations or mistakes made with those people can disqualify potential police officers. Being a successful police officer starts in patrol. Your first three to five years are where you make your mark. The community you will serve needs to know you as a constant stabilizing presence when you are on duty. Victims of crime and witnesses to those crimes need to believe they can trust you in times of crisis. None of this occurs without hard work and genuine demonstrated empathy by police officers.

Your role as a police officer is not about you. Do the minor calls, even if they are repetitive and boring. Do them with the same thoroughness and attention to detail you would if you were at a major crime scene. Until you are actually a victim of a crime, no matter how minor, as a police officer it's hard to understand the frustration of victims. I dealt with many victims of crimes over the years and what they want from you as a police officer is quite simple. They want reassurance and leadership, even if the crime is fairly minor in the overall scheme of things.

For example, I used to get annoyed with having to take reports of stolen bicycles until my son's bicycle was stolen while he was swimming at a civic centre. We had budgeted and saved to get him the bike and, until it was stolen, I had never really given a lot of thought to the impact that a relatively minor theft had on the victims. My son lost his mobility and we had to scramble to get him a new one. Not the case of the century or anything like that, but the crime affected our quality of life. I immediately felt bad for the many times I had quickly taken reports from complainants with barely disguised annoyance. They had bothered me, "the important police officer with better things to do," to report their minor problem. But it wasn't minor to them.

Another piece of advice would be to deal with young offenders, even if you think nothing will happen to them in court. During their first encounter with the police, you may make the difference between that young offender being just a kid who made a mistake and their launching into a life of crime. Deal with the traffic matters and impaired drivers, even if you know you will spend hours in court and, god forbid, the offender is found not guilty. This is where you learn your trade. This is where you hone your skills. You are a leader, whether or not you thought you were before you entered into policing. It's inescapable. So be the best leader you can be.

Report writing is a huge part of policing. A report you file is a living document. It has to convey what happened at an incident to people who were not there but still have to act upon the report. Depending on the incident, it can be read many times by many different people for years to come. Lawyers, parole or probation officers, insurance agents, academics—the possibilities are endless. With increasing access to information requests and ever-changing rules, you never know where your report will end up, so file good reports.

I used to joke that I didn't care where the ammunition and gas came from as long as I had it when I was working. I don't do that when I talk to police recruits. I tell them to network with all of the emergency services and to learn where the resources come from. I wish I had been told this earlier on in my career. It's always beneficial to know how the organization you work for functions.

Mastering the basics is the foundation of all good police officers. I cover the above-mentioned subjects and more in the two hours I am given when speaking to recruits or young constables. I know they are covered many times over through more formal sessions before the officers graduate. Leadership, empathy, and commitment cannot be overemphasized to young officers. Checking your ego and realizing who you are there to serve and protect will give you a fulfilling and rewarding career. I feel honoured to have the opportunity to tell them some of what I have learned.

CHAPTER 7
STREET CHECKS, COURT ORDERS, AND COMMUNITY POLICING

I learned some very important lessons from the very beginning of my career in the Saskatoon Police, and they applied for the rest of my career. You could say they are at the centre of all good policing.

Every police officer, from the youngest patrol officer to the most seasoned homicide investigator, will tell you the same thing. From serial killings to routine vandalism, many of these crimes have been solved because another police officer had contact with a person and recorded their particulars. Recorded contacts are the cornerstone of effective community policing. Failing to record contacts with civilians has cost some police officers their jobs.

I have conducted thousands of these street checks over the course of my career. It was a huge part of what made me an effective police officer. I wanted to know who was in the areas I worked and if they were involved in criminal activity. A good district officer was an asset to the community he worked in. The citizens expected the constable in their community to be on top of things—that is unless they were criminals themselves.

Somehow, in the past few years, street checks have become a flashpoint issue. Police officers are being accused of abusing their authority and of racial profiling while conducting the business of community policing. Some jurisdictions have introduced legislation to regulate how a police officer and a citizen can interact in the first few seconds of police contact. These laws or regulations are on top of the Charter of Rights legislation already in place as the law of our land.

These new rules remind me of the United Nations' Rules of Engagement (ROE) for Canadian Forces peacekeeping missions when I was in Cyprus in the early '80s. According to the United Nations' ROE, we weren't to carry more than twenty rounds of ammunition for our personal weapons. The weapon could have the magazine attached but no round in the chamber. If we were engaged, we were to announce that we were United Nations peacekeepers and were not to engage a threat unless we were fired upon. If fired upon, we were supposed to fire two warning shots, only engage the identified leader, and, if possible, shoot them in the legs. These rules were created by someone—to a soldier's mind, at least—who had obviously never been in situations like the ones peacekeepers encountered on their missions. The rules were printed on a card or printed in an aide-mémoire (a small manual) and were either supposed to be memorized or carried. I kept my card under my field dressing. A field dressing was a large bandage in a waterproof package designed to allow a soldier to dress a large wound like a gunshot or shrapnel wound. I did this because I knew I would need the bandage long before I would need the card.

These rules have been proven ineffective time and time again as the nature of peacekeeping has changed to stopping wars. The cost has been enormous to people in conflict zones. The UN's reputation as an organization able to stop conflict and monitor peace has suffered accordingly. I am not comparing policing to peacekeeping in a war zone. Policing is, however, peacekeeping. Many First Nations, for example, call their police services peacekeepers.

Drawing on my military experience—the military tends to be a little blunter about these things—I would ask, when it comes to policing the streets, what is the mission? And what is the desired outcome when police are doing their work on the streets and in our communities? Over the years, I watched my own police leaders struggle with these questions. The communities I worked in wanted police officers to be accessible, approachable, and available. At the same time, they wanted us to deal with gangs, drug dealers, and criminals who affected their quality of life. Basically, law-abiding people in the areas I worked wanted peace. So keeping people safe and maintaining order became my mission.

To accomplish my mission, I needed to know who was who. How I did that was by checking people I didn't know. If they were in places or situations where the vast majority of the other community members were normally not, I would check them. Many of the street checks I conducted led to relationship building, and many led to arrests. Many of the checks allowed me to defuse violent situations in later encounters with the people I had dealt with while doing the checks.

I found that the people where I worked wanted to know the police officers who were dealing with them or their relations. They wanted to understand you as a person. Since leaving policing, I have heard many times from people, "This cop is a good guy," or "You need to stay out of that officer's way because he is all business." People want the tangible, and when there is a measure of understanding between people in the community and the police, it encourages peace. The vast majority of violent encounters I had were with people who didn't know me, or I didn't know them. The majority of bad outcomes when police and citizens interact come from not knowing each other.

In our highly mobile society it is inevitable that there will be some police and stranger contacts. The majority of police and citizen encounters happen in their respective home communities. The majority of these encounters are peaceful or semi-peaceful, even if they result in an arrest. Street checks and the police officer's ability to conduct them within the structure of the current laws are what allow these encounters to happen without incident. If the police get it wrong, there are plenty of lawyers and a court system that will tell them so.

Ironically, those who say they're trying to reduce violent encounters between police officers and citizens by attempting to restrict the ability of police officers to conduct street checks on people they don't know actually *increases* the likelihood of those types of incidents occurring. For example, when a street gang or criminal organization tries to dominate an ethnic community, and they identify themselves by their ethnicity as part of their criminal identity, they increase the likelihood of noncriminal members of their community being checked by the police. At the same time, the main question that people who are affected by crime ask is, "Why aren't the police doing something about the criminals, drugs, and violence?" Fewer street checks can mean a lessened ability by police to answer that question.

When I served as a police officer, the people I was checking often accused me of being "racist." Because I'm Indigenous, I would be accused of "working against my own people." In my experience, the majority of those who accused me of racism had outstanding criminal warrants or were breaking the law. I didn't blame them. The best defence is a good offence when you're trying to avoid getting arrested. In my world, huge red flags went up whenever a person called a street check racially motivated.

That being said, there is no doubt some police officers lack the tact or experience to conduct street checks and establish a working relationship with citizens in the areas they work. There are officers who make no attempt to learn about the people they police. I have dealt with and worked with officers who had racist views. I have also dealt with citizens and criminals who had racist views.

There are two distinct groups among problem police officers. The first includes those who believe and harbour racist viewpoints and never act upon them. They reveal themselves through a careless comment or frustration with a situation. The second group practises what they believe. A single police officer in this second group can undo the good work of a thousand other officers in a heartbeat. The actions and inactions of some of the investigators and their supervisors during the investigation into the freezing death of Neil Stonechild in Saskatchewan stand out as one of the most glaring examples. The subsequent inquiry into his death hammered home the importance of accountability and the need to eliminate racial bias within police services across Canada.

This where diversity in the makeup of a police service can have the most impact on the conduct of police officers in contact with minorities. While serving, I learned every day from working with men and women with totally different backgrounds and experiences. I learned about their beliefs and values. I didn't always agree, but I learned.

The people who are the least affected by crime and have the least contact with police officers are often the harshest critics of the police. They have their place and are entitled to their opinions. However, there were times in my career when their rhetoric almost made me feel like I was part of an oppressive force actively seeking to trample the rights and liberties of others. (I hoped my family didn't think I was an armed thug working with racists to violate people's rights). Social activists have a role to play in making our society and police services better. However, sometimes the passion of social justice advocates outstrips the facts and realities of interactions between the police and the majority of community members in some areas in Canada.

Could a change in language assuage the people who are offended by the police doing street checks? I think it's been tried in some jurisdictions; I know we called street checks "community initiatives" at one time in Saskatoon. Whatever the terminology used, it still involves the physical act of asking and recording people's names and information. It all falls under the umbrella of community policing.

Whenever a police officer and a citizen interact, there is always a take-away. It is true of all human interactions. The take-away, if you are not a criminal, is entirely up to the person being checked. You can be offended or feel you have been wronged. Or you can take away a bit of understanding about how police solve crimes and keep an area safe. The first five to ten seconds are always the most tension-filled for the officer and the person being checked. There will never be a perfect system for conducting street checks, but it still has to be done.

In one cynical early phase of my career, I used to joke that there were three classes of people for the patrolman: suspects, victims, and witnesses. Conducting street checks regularly over a long career and making other kinds of contacts cured me of that cynicism, though. It allowed me to see and appreciate the people where I worked as...people.

To restrict or take away the ability of police officers to talk to people—which is a hot item on the political agenda these days—also takes away the responsibility of the young officer, especially, to learn tact and diplomacy. It also allows criminals to simply walk away from police officers. And many interactions would become impersonal and system-driven, and those are the most dangerous interactions for citizens and police officers alike. In my opinion, the changes and proposed changes to how police conduct checks are a step backward for police and community relations.

Enforcing court orders—another big part of my workload during my career—goes hand in hand with street checks. Court orders effectively protect the public from unrepentant criminals who aren't ready to stop breaking the law. They work in countless different scenarios. If the police in the course of their duties cannot question people, how are they to learn if someone is accused before the courts of a crime or any number of crimes? A child sex offender could walk freely in an area frequented by children, even if he had conditions not to be in such an area, if the police are restricted from even asking his name.

Some would have the police unable to access information on court orders until offenders commit a new crime, making existing court orders ineffective. "System-generated charges for petty crimes" is how defence lawyers and social justice advocates describe the enforcement of court-ordered conditions by police involving an accused person freed while awaiting trial. The argument is that, by enforcing court orders, the police are marginalizing youth and other people by making them feel they are not a part of mainstream society. Calling it reactive policing, some people clamour to minimize the ability of the police to enforce court orders and conduct street checks. However, rather than being merely reactive policing, enforcing court orders is *proactive* policing.

When I was a police officer, I laid thousands of breach charges. I saw the value of enforcing the orders of the courts early on in my career. In cases of domestic violence, drug trafficking, and other crimes against people, enforcing court orders was invaluable in stopping the offender's behaviour.

When a person is charged or convicted of an offence in Canada, many alternatives are available to the courts. While awaiting trial, a person can be released on their own recognizance with a promise they will return to court on an agreed-upon date. If the charge is more serious, after a hearing a person may be released on an undertaking, which has conditions the accused must abide by so they can be released from custody while awaiting trial. Depending on the person's record, they may be as simple as requiring the accused to keep the peace, be of good behaviour, and attend court when ordered.

Some accused will have stricter conditions, such as sticking to a curfew and abstaining from alcohol or drugs, to try to keep them out of custody prior to their trial. Even after a conviction for an offence, there are myriad alternative sentences available to the courts to keep someone from going to jail. Probation is one of the better-known examples, but another is implementing a conditional sentence order (CSO).

A CSO occurs when a sentence is passed after a guilty conviction or guilty plea. The offender is sentenced to a jail term but doesn't actually go to jail. They are released on conditions, and if they abide by those conditions during the length of their sentence, they will not go to jail. Theoretically, if they breach the conditions, they will be taken back into custody and serve the remainder of their sentence in prison. As a police officer, I used to joke that CSOs were "double serious probation."

Every alternative release or pre-trial release has some sort of conditions attached to it. An accused or convicted person signs the conditions before they are released. They swear they will abide by the conditions and give their word to gain their release. Some people take the conditions seriously, and a great many abide by all of the conditions until the matter before the courts is resolved.

However, there are others who do not comply and start to breach their conditions as soon as they are out of sight of the courthouse. I have seen convicted impaired drivers driving within two hours of their convictions. Men who assaulted their spouses have been picked up after seeing the very people they were ordered to have no contact with. And accused drug dealers have been picked up after consorting with active drug dealers and gang members and using cellphones, even when prohibited from doing so.

On one occasion early in my career, I arrested a parolee who had been released from the penitentiary in Prince Albert, Saskatchewan. He was released in Prince Albert and put on a bus to Saskatoon. From the bus depot, he went straight to the bar in violation of his parole and he was re-arrested. His freedom lasted a total of six hours.

I once arrested three men for a brutal sexual assault just a week before Christmas, and they were released on conditions not to associate with each other or consume alcohol. On my first day back on duty, I went to check on one of the accused to ensure he was abiding by his conditions. I found all three men together, drinking before lunch hour. After arresting them all, they ended up back in custody, in remand until the trial.

Remand is quite simply when you are kept in jail while you await trial because your continued presence in the community is considered too much of a risk to the general public. Remand can be and has been controversial for people awaiting trial, and many of the prisoners in provincial custody are there on remand. Sometimes a person cannot meet the bail conditions imposed by the courts to obtain their release. Here is where the power of money can tip the scales of justice against a person who lacks financial resources. Some criminals like drug dealers and gang members have the money to post large bail amounts. They will promise whatever it takes to secure their release so they can get back to business.

Some people have built up such lengthy records for failing to attend court or failing to abide by court-ordered conditions that they have lost the trust of the courts. Sadly, some offenders have no support systems like a home or family who can take pre-trial custody of them. They end up languishing in remand due to a variety of social and legal reasons. Whatever the circumstance, when a person becomes involved in the criminal justice system as an accused, the onus is on them to comply with pre-trial release conditions and not commit new crimes while on a judicial release. The court's and the Crown prosecutor's primary duty at the outset is to protect the general public from criminal behaviour.

When I first started with the Saskatoon Police, breaching people for violating court-ordered conditions was looked down upon. The corporals in the detention area where prisoners were booked would ask what the charges were for each prisoner. When I would list three counts of breaching an undertaking or a single count of breach of probation, they would ask, "But what charge is he in for?" They were expecting a new charge, like theft or assault, as if a breach of court orders wasn't serious enough to book the prisoner.

It took a lot of explanation to get people to see my reasoning for enforcing court orders. Everyone from the detention corporals to the central records personnel who had to type the reports questioned the value of breaching suspects for violation of court orders. It definitely created a lot of work for other people. From the detention staff to the clerks at the courts and everyone involved in the system, breach arrests increased their workloads.

It came to a head when my partner told me other patrol officers were angry and were talking disparagingly about my policing methods. I expected that from some people, but hearing it from my peers in patrol really stung. We went to an up-and-coming Crown prosecutor, who I greatly respected, and asked him if the arrests had value to the courts. He eloquently explained that the arrests and enforcement of court orders had great value to the Crown, as long as we didn't place too high of a value or stake on the outcome of each individual case. We were establishing the individual criminal's credibility to abide by the conditions of the court if they were released pre-trial. If an active criminal was constantly in violation of court-ordered release conditions while awaiting trial on a serious offence, it was easier to have them kept in custody until their trial.

When a person is arrested for an offence for which the Criminal Code of Canada stipulates the accused must attend court in order to be released from custody, their arrest triggers a whole series of processes. The initial arrest generates an arrest report. The arrest report details the incident, and added to the arrest report is the accused's criminal record. When the accused arrives at court, often with many other arrests, a Crown prosecutor who is assigned to the morning dockets has to read the report and decide if the accused can be released without risk to the public. They also have to decide what they must do to ensure the accused will return to court to answer to their charge. If the Crown opposes the release of an accused, the accused is entitled to a hearing. The hearing is called a show cause hearing. The Crown has to show cause to keep the accused in custody. This is where breach charges laid by the police assist the prosecutors by showing the propensity of the suspect to disregard orders of the court.

In the majority of show cause hearings, rarely are witnesses called and the records of the accused, as well as the seriousness of the offence, will decide whether the accused is released. I only testified at one show cause hearing in my entire career. It involved a man who had stabbed his common law wife in the throat after a domestic dispute. Even though her wounds had been life-threatening, she was less than co-operative. Her husband, a hardened career criminal, was arrested. He was sitting in the back of my patrol car while I was making notes. I reread him his charges, advised him of his rights, and asked him if he understood. He responded with a profanity, adding, "Yeah? So, what? She won't testify."

I wanted another witness to that very telling utterance, so I switched the radio to a secondary channel. I keyed the radio microphone and asked the accused to repeat himself. He did. I asked the dispatcher if he had heard the accused. He replied, "10-4." I asked him to mark the time, so the recording could be recovered.

This was a new tactic for me. Back in the early '90s, patrol cars weren't wired the way they are now. The electronic audio capture of interactions between the accused and patrol officers was a relatively unexplored area in Saskatchewan. The courts would have the final say as to whether his utterance would be heard as evidence. I transported the accused to detention and he was booked in.

He made his first court appearance in the morning and was remanded for a show cause hearing the following morning. The following morning was the end of my night shift. I was contacted by the Crown prosecutor and told the defence lawyer who had taken the case had asked for a rarely used hearing called a viva voce motion. The Crown lawyer explained that a viva voce motion was a show cause hearing where the accused seeks to be "freed by voice" or testimony called at the hearing. The initial reason for holding the show cause hearing is that the facts are in dispute between the defence lawyer and the Crown to the disadvantage of the accused. The victim was denying her throat was cut by the accused, and the accused was denying his utterance.

I arrived at the court after my night shift and waited all day to testify. I could barely keep my eyes open by 10:00 a.m. as the legal arguments over what testimony would be allowed went on. They went on until 5:00 p.m. I never did testify and the accused was held in custody and ultimately pleaded guilty to a lesser charge.

I decided to let policy catch up to innovation and, though many utterances were captured during radio communications afterwards, I never tried to introduce them as evidence unless I was asked to do so. The present systems allow for many of the interactions between patrol officers and the accused to be recorded. The courts have come to expect there will be film and audio for them to review. I like the new way better than what we used to do.

I could see over the years there were inequalities in the system when it came to the alleged offender's ability to secure bail or a judicial release prior to their trial. The tricky balance of race, education, and income made the justice system and the police enforcing court orders appear unbalanced. For some First Nations people, being remanded into custody after an arrest seemed a foregone conclusion. This was especially true for people from northern communities who had built up a record of failing to attend court because the difficulties of travelling from their home communities seemed insurmountable.

So they just let charges go to warrants and let the police transport them. I think this will become less prevalent as time passes, as people are now more educated and there is more access to information technology.

Public education will and has made a difference in how people navigate the legal system. There are criminals—regardless of race, income, or education—who manipulate the system or simply have no respect for the courts. There are some who string out court appearances, hoping witnesses will just get tired of coming to court. Other more serious criminals will attempt to contact witnesses to intimidate, dissuade, or harm them prior to trial once they have obtained a judicial release on a charge. Organized criminals and street gangs can and do use pre-trial release to get things done in their favour.

Enforcing court orders in cases of domestic violence is one of the areas where police should always be vigilant. There have been way too many murders of women by abusive men who were out on some sort of judicial release for offences committed against those very same women they have murdered. Often the police and courts will be subject to criticism and be questioned on why the protective orders were not enforced or why violations were dealt with the way they were.

Street checks and the enforcement of court orders are not a system-driven criminalization of citizens, or an indicator of racism. Instead, these are simply tools employed by the justice system that promote accountability, wise personal choices, and responsibility among people who need to be constantly reminded of these things, all the while protecting the rest of us.

CHAPTER 8
BRINKSMANSHIP–
THE USE OF FORCE, PART 2

A few chapters ago, I was writing about the use of force, which has been an issue for me going back to my days as a young soldier peacekeeping in Cyprus. Unavoidably, for anyone as involved in policing as I subsequently was, it's been a big issue ever since. Consequently, I've got more to share with you.

The police, and their use of force to stop crime or apprehend criminals, have never been under more scrutiny than in the past few years. I have used force many times in the course of my career. There are times when there is no other alternative.

Words have failed, the subject is actively assaulting a citizen—or you—or is armed with an intent to injure: these are all situations where using force is all you have left. You have to react quickly and decisively. You stop the threat and try not to injure the suspect. Underreact and someone, including police officers, will pay the price. Knowing how and when to intervene is the challenge. I know police officers often have only five to ten seconds to make a decision about how to react in a violent encounter with a suspect.

While still in training as a rookie cop, I went to a call with my FTO, where there was a domestic assault and the estranged husband had caused some damage to the home. My trainer took the lead and arrested the suspect. We escorted him to our patrol car, and the trainer told me to watch the suspect while he took a written statement from the victim. I wasn't used to not being in charge, so I stood outside the car and waited for my FTO to come back. The arrested male was extremely agitated, swearing and protesting his innocence. He must have sensed I was new to the Saskatoon Police because he called me a rookie and began kicking at the side windows. Using both feet, he would soon have broken the window and gotten out.

I wasn't used to working with a partner on a day shift, so I didn't bother to call my training officer on the radio. I was just waiting for the window to break so I could deal with him when he got out. The suspect caused enough of a commotion that my trainer must have heard it because he rushed out of the house. He angrily told me that, as a civilian police officer, you didn't wait until the situation was out of hand before you called for backup. I had underreacted and the suspect had tried to take advantage of it. He settled down once there were two of us. He was transported to jail without incident.

Appropriate reaction, overreaction, and underreaction to violence would be constant themes and would invoke a never-ending, day-to-day decision process for me throughout my career. When I was a military police officer, it all seemed pretty clear and, because I often worked alone, I just made the decision and acted on it. In the civilian world there were many new variables that I had never considered. Military personnel have many common values, even when they are in conflict with the law. This often put limits on potentially explosive situations. In the civilian world the field was wide open. A suspect could kill or injure you and escape without consequences, if they successfully got away.

I have talked about many violent situations in my first two books. There is no shortage of stories to tell. It wasn't until I had left policing and patrol work that I realized what a violent life I had lived. As the years passed, and I gained experience, I knew when to use force and when to back off. In spite of my experience, I still made mistakes. Instincts and experience can only carry you so far in patrol work and policing. You can become overconfident or begin to doubt yourself.

One night, several patrol cars attended to a noisy party. When we arrived, there was one male at the party who I knew as an extremely violent individual. He was baiting us, saying we had no right to be there and to just "fuck off!" and leave them alone. He wouldn't step off the property where I could deal with him. I was cocky—he had gotten under my skin and I called him a coward, baiting him. The exchange became heated and I lost perspective. I wanted him to come off the property, so I could arrest him, and if it turned into a fight, so much the better. He wanted me to come on the property with the same mindset. Another constable intervened and calmed things down. She got me out of there and the man's friends got him in the house. The party host peacefully took the ticket for excessive noise.

It was an overreaction. I let my personal feelings for the man cloud my judgment. I was ready to fight and arrest this man because I knew how dangerous he was. It was the wrong time and the wrong place to force an encounter. My colleague was right to intervene, but a couple of months later that same man beat someone so badly he ended up in the penitentiary.

The use of force is the greatest test of a police officer's professionalism: just because you can doesn't always mean you should. There were many instances in my career where I had passed the legal threshold of justified use of force, where morally, for me, it would have seemed punitive. Resisting the urge to mete out justice by using force on a suspect who has inflicted pain on someone else is what defines a professional, well-trained police officer. Controlling your emotions when dealing with violent people and the aftermath of their crimes is a never-ending challenge as you go through your career. Police-themed movies and television shows are entertainment only when the subject matter is police using force to get revenge or to serve a criminal his just desserts.

There are now many professions where second-guessing everything you do has become an everyday occurrence. Politicians, medical professionals, athletes, and doctors find themselves being second-guessed. Police officers, corrections officers, lawyers, and judges make decisions with the certain knowledge everything will be scrutinized, tried, or appealed.

I responded once to a domestic assault-in-progress call. As I approached the apartment door, I could hear the very distinctive and disturbing sound of a fist striking flesh. The apartment door was unlocked. When I pushed it open, the suspect was holding his spouse by the hair and was just cocking his fist to hit her again. Reacting, I punched him in the face as he turned to look at me. He slumped into the wall and I handcuffed him. It was not a textbook use of force, and on video it would have looked ugly. But it was effective and it ended the assault. He pleaded guilty at trial and the punch was never brought up. Knowing when to act and end violence by using force is a balancing act for every officer. There were many times over the course of my policing career when using force was timely and appropriate. Yet every time it was ugly and looked exactly like what it was—the use of violence to stop violence.

In every modern and professional police service, the use of force is recorded and correlated. The lessons learned from each encounter are incorporated into future training. What cannot be fit into training scenarios is experience. Experience helps to reduce the shock of seeing raw violence and helps an officer formulate the appropriate response quicker. The human factor will always be an element of so-called police violence.

When police officers react to violence and use force to effect an arrest, they bring all of the emotions we all have with them. If they are afraid, frustrated, tired, or injured, it can have an influence on how an arrest comes to a conclusion. All those and many other emotions can colour a justified use of force into what people call "police violence."

The use of force by police has been and always will be a contentious issue for our society. There are times when there is no question the police were compelled to act, and the public backs them completely. An example would be a shootout with a murderer who opens fire on police, or a suspect who is threatening hostages with death in a kidnapping situation. It is the other 99 percent of situations the public knows nothing about where officers decide in five to ten seconds where the brink is and act. It is where the majority of risk is inherited and where experience, training, and common sense can save lives.

I know from my own experience. I know from working with many fine women and men over the years. Police don't go to work and look for opportunities to use force. They don't go looking for fights and ways to hurt people. Unfortunately, they have to be ready and able to react if they are forced to protect the public and themselves.

CHAPTER 9
POLICE AND THE SURVIVORS OF SEXUAL ASSAULT

In the years since I left policing, there's been a constant stream of stories in the media about sexual violence. A lot of this coverage is sensationalist and troubling. Overall, though, being more open about discussing sex crimes is probably a good thing, because crime is crime and all aspects of criminal justice deserve open discussion.

It gets more complicated, though, with the controversial, high-profile cases. Like the time a prominent CBC radio personality was accused of sexual assault, and was charged, tried, and ultimately acquitted, which enraged many people. High-decibel opinions expressed for and against him in social and mainstream media seemed high on outrage and low on facts to a veteran police officer like me. Facts, however, were what I dealt with when investigating sex crimes over the whole of my career.

Some critics say there's no use in victims reporting sex crimes because the system is so flawed that justice isn't achievable. For example, the widely reported case of a judge asking a teenage victim of sexual assault why she couldn't keep her knees together certainly doesn't give victims a lot of hope. There have been stories of places like universities and colleges not acting on complaints of sexual violence until they were exposed in the media. And the statistics that consistently show the relatively low conviction rate of people accused of sexual violence still shock me. I can see where the anger and frustration are coming from. Because of my policing career, I'm all too aware of the prevalence of sexual violence in our society.

The palpable pain and frustration of victims of sexual violence that I personally witnessed over and over again will forever be imprinted on my mind. The uncontrollable shaking, the screams of rage, the drawing up of limbs to make a shield against further pain are things you just never forget. As a male police officer, I also often found myself at a loss as to what to do to help the mostly female victims of sexual violence with whom I dealt. But it was my duty to help them to the best of my ability.

Every victim was different too. For some, the reported crime I was dealing with may not have been their first experience with sexual violence. They may have been victims of incest, or date rape unreported in the past, which just deepened the trauma of their latest assault. When a uniformed officer, like I was for the whole my career, is called to the scene of one of these crimes, the offence is almost always fresh and like a raw, open wound to the victim. And this initial contact with the victim is pivotal to everything that happens afterwards.

It has to be recognized that police officers bring all of their life experiences—all of their personal values, good and bad—to a call like this, because, especially if we're men, we are fathers, husbands, brothers, and sons. We're also all fallible human beings. But if a victim feels the investigating officers are judging them for their lifestyles or choices, you might as well do what we called, "clear the call and go back in service." In other words, leave, because the victim isn't going to cooperate if she feels unsupported by you.

A police officer's job, then, when making the first contact with a reported sexual assault victim, is to listen and observe, withholding judgment as much as possible. In addition to opening that channel of communication with the victim, if this contact is at the scene of the crime, preservation of physical evidence must be a priority. More often than not, though, the contact is at the hospital, where the victim is receiving treatment. But the same consideration of preservation of evidence occurs there too.

Some victims are animated, angry, and ready to tell you what happened. Others are almost catatonic and have to be gently pressed to relate what occurred. Yet others oscillate back and forth between these states. Police officers, therefore, have to remember to be flexible and to expect that the victim will shut down and come back several times during an interview. Typically, the victim doesn't understand the police officer's role. The complexity of the law and rules of evidence mean nothing to them. What they need, though, is for you to listen to them respectfully.

Yet a police officer also can never forget what they need to do when investigating these crimes. When I read the statistics on conviction rates, and looked at my own experiences, I wondered why the chances of success in solving the crimes were so low. I now better understand that the earlier the victim reports being assaulted, the better the chances of recovering physical evidence, in particular the DNA of their attacker. Also, the sooner an assault is reported, the better the chances of having witnesses who can corroborate the victim's account of events. Having a witness who can soon after an assault recount the conversations and actions occurring between the victim and the attacker can be crucial to the case when it goes to trial.

When I first started with the Saskatoon Police in 1987, DNA evidence was still years away from being introduced and accepted in Canadian courtrooms. Sexual assault evidence, such as bodily fluids and clothing, could, at best, be blood-typed. Even if you could get a blood sample from the suspect, there was no certainty of conviction. A suspect's blood could be similar but not specific enough to obtain a conviction on blood alone.

As patrolmen, we didn't receive a whole lot of specific training for investigating sex crimes. We received more information on what not to do than what to do. We were told about all the agencies that could assist us, like the sexual assault centres. In hindsight, given the high rate of sexual violence, reported and unreported, there most definitely needed to be more training back in my day. And it wouldn't hurt to step up training in investigating sex crimes in today's police colleges as well.

Modern-day technologies, like the DNA analysis now used in investigating sex crimes, are a quantum leap over what I had back in my early police days. What hasn't changed, though, is the next most important part of the initial investigation of a complaint of sexual assault: the interview.

The area I worked in Saskatoon for most of my career had a high rate of violent crime. Many of the local residents were poor and, with the issues that come with poverty, were forced to live with levels of violence people in more affluent areas in the city would never have tolerated. Racism and sexual violence were closely linked in the cases I encountered early in my career. I think the perpetrators (of all ethnic backgrounds) that I arrested early in my career never expected their victims to report the crimes and, when they did, they never expected the victims to follow through on those complaints.

Indigenous women where I worked were the most exploited and frequent victims of criminals and sexual offenders. A lot of victims didn't have confidence or trust in the justice system and were highly suspicious of the police. This was understandable because, even as late as the early '90s, thanks to the legacy of residential schools, the '60s Scoop, and other injustices, women in this community who were victims of sexual violence didn't think anyone would listen, or, if they did, that they'd be believed. And, like a lot of victims of sexual violence, many of these women believed they had somehow brought it upon themselves.

Early in my career, I responded to a call of a sexual assault at a home. The woman hadn't gone to the hospital. She was a couple of years older than I was at the time. She was angry and very quickly torn on whether she should have reported the assault at all. She began qualifying her account, very quickly blaming herself for accepting an offer from an acquaintance to share a few beers. After having a few drinks, the man sexually assaulted her. Following the attack, he threatened to torture her with a broken light bulb if she dared call the police, yet she was brave enough to call us.

I reminded her that it wasn't her fault and that I wasn't going to judge her on the events leading up to the attack. I was still pretty new, but her account was straightforward, and I believed her. She had nothing to gain by making a false report. In spite of everything she had been through, she was willing to give a written statement. She identified her rapist from a photo lineup and I located and arrested him.

He expressed disbelief that she had reported the assault. He was a Caucasian man from the generation that still used the word "squaw" and every other racist term to describe his accuser. He didn't deny the assault, but he didn't admit to it either. I think he was totally shocked that an Indigenous woman had accused him and that an Indigenous police officer had arrested him. He pled guilty at his first court appearance and received a substantial prison sentence.

I don't think a case like this, even as straightforward as it was at the time, would be resolved so simply now. Victim testimony, witness statements, photo lineups, and blood typing of bodily fluids don't hold as much weight for the Crown prosecutors, defence lawyers, and the courts as they used to. DNA, a very specific genetic marker so unique to an individual as to exclude its donor from everyone else in society, has become the silver bullet in many sexual assault cases. But DNA can be explained away if the suspect and victim had previous relations, or in date rape, he-said-she-said cases. Even with the advances in science and evidence collection, I still firmly believe that something as simple and elementary as the first contact and the follow-up interview remain the most crucial parts of the investigation of sexual assaults.

Reading the media reporting of high-profile sexual assault trials, I can understand the frustration of victims. But I cannot imagine the anger and hopelessness some victims feel if their alleged attacker is acquitted. As the initial investigator—and sometimes the only investigator—of many sexual assaults, I took some satisfaction when the offender pleaded out or was found guilty. Many of the victims thanked me for believing in them. I also believe the Crown prosecutors got convictions because the victims told the complete truth and believed in themselves and saw their own value. Meanwhile, we have to remember that polarized and expressed opinions in the mainstream and social media concerning high-profile sexual violence cases are not the facts.

Changing a culture where sexual violence is accepted is difficult. Each case is a personal journey for the victims. In my parents' generation in northern Ontario, there were many unreported sexual crimes. The victims suffered in silence, and the suffering manifested itself in addictions, mental health problems, and encounters with the law. I can't imagine it was different in many other places in Canada. Somehow, incomprehensibly to me as a man and a police officer, this was, and still is, the reality for some victims. Things have to change, and perhaps they are changing as we talk more openly about sexual violence. I can only hope I did my duty with empathy and compassion for the victims I encountered over the years.

CHAPTER 10
YOU ARE OFF DUTY...
SO WHAT SHOULD YOU DO?

When you are off duty as a police officer, you have a bit of anonymity depending on the size of your community. RCMP officers and small-town police department members are in a more difficult spot because almost everyone knows who they are. Saskatoon is somewhere in between because the longer you are a police officer, the better known you become depending on your assignment.

In my case, the Saskatoon Police Department, as it was called in 1988, wanted to show it was attempting to be more inclusive and diverse. As part of this initiative, the *Saskatoon StarPhoenix* interviewed me, along with another Indigenous officer. The article, including our photos, was intended to attract more Aboriginal recruits. Being a fairly new guy, I went along with the department because I didn't think saying no was an option. More experienced officers told me I was blowing my chances of working undercover in the future. At that point in my career I wasn't even thinking along those lines.

After the article was published, I was invited to talk at schools and some functions at the behest of the school and community liaison officers and, being the good soldier, I went along with the requests. It got to be too much very quickly, though, as I was still learning how to be a police officer. Once I had enough time and experience under my belt, I began to say no to public speaking requests. It was a combination of things that led me away from being more community-involved in the early stages of my career. The crime rate was high and the other officers from my shift had to cover my area while I was doing the "soft jobs." This caused some resentment, which doesn't make things any easier when you're trying to fit in. Justified or not, the resentment of your peers can be a strong motivator in making you a team player. I also felt I didn't have the experience to make a difference.

In spite of being seen by a lot of people in a short period of time, I could still move around the downtown of Saskatoon without being recognized as a police officer. I was, however, a police officer. I thought like a police officer and, as most new guys do, acted like a police officer. Little things like making direct eye contact when approaching unknown people, always looking for threats, and quickly scanning every room I entered became part of my persona. It's almost funny to think about it now, but it was part of the process every new officer goes through to some extent.

When you are off duty and you see a criminal act, the way you react is as individual as the officer. You can call it in and act like any other civilian witness until the police who are working arrive to take control. You can intervene, make the arrest, and then call it in. Or you can walk away, using whatever rationale allows you to. The seriousness of the crime sometimes dictates what an off-duty officer will do. All arrest situations have the potential to be dangerous. Making off-duty arrests are especially dangerous. When you are on duty, you are mentally prepared for confrontation and making arrests. You are fully equipped and in communication with your co-workers. When you are off duty, this is usually not the case. You may be grocery shopping or taking your children to school, but you are not looking for trouble.

When I was working, there was no clear policy or directives by the administration for what to do when you saw crimes occur while off duty. The area where this was and is difficult for off-duty officers is liability. If an off-duty officer sees an offence and doesn't intervene, and a citizen recognizes the police officer, can the citizen legitimately complain that the officer has neglected their duty? What will the media, or a lawyer, do with the information? It's a tough place to be when you're a police officer.

On one hand, you give it your all when you're working and just want to be a husband, wife, and parent when you're not. On the other hand, you have the moral, and arguably the legal, obligation as a trained police officer to protect and serve, whether you are working or not. This is part of the reason I have great respect for the RCMP, Ontario Provincial Police, Sûreté du Québec, and all the other officers who work in small detachments throughout Canada. They are always on the clock when they are in their assigned communities.

During my career with the Saskatoon Police, I knew of four officers who were seriously injured as a result of assaults while intervening in criminal situations while off duty. The attackers, once they knew the officers were off duty and alone, increased the ferocity of the assaults accordingly. It would make any police officer wary of getting involved in anything when they're not working.

My first two off-duty arrests were early in my career and in the pre-cellular phone era. They were both for drug trafficking when I lived in Saskatoon's downtown. After I met my fiancé and we moved to our own house, I thought that being out of the higher crime areas would let me just be a citizen on my days off. I had been the subject of another newspaper article and had taken two CBC reporters on patrol with me for different stories they were covering. One story was featured on *The National* and had been picked up by CNN. It was getting harder to move around Saskatoon without someone looking at me and wondering where they knew me from. Fortunately, except for the most astute people, the average person, unless it directly affects them, moves on quickly and you go back to being just a guy.

One day I left home to go for a run. It was a beautiful summer day and, as anyone can attest, people drive faster when the weather gets nice. I was running on a busy street when I heard two motorcycles open up their throttles behind me. Even with my headphones on, and the music cranked up, it was thunderous. They were racing and flew by me at a very high rate of speed. One motorcycle was a traditional chopper and the other a sport bike where the driver is hunched forward. We used to call them crotch rockets. Even if I had been working and driving a patrol car, I would have never caught them. I saw them turn onto a main street that runs east and west across the entire east side of Saskatoon. I thought to myself, those guys are going to kill themselves.

I kept running and turned onto the street they had turned onto and saw two cars with their four-way flashers going and a crowd of people coming off the adjacent golf course. The two motorcycles had apparently touched foot pegs and the sport bike lost control. The motorcycle and rider slid into a street lamp. The rider, in spite of wearing a helmet, had contacted the street lamp and was killed. Sweaty, wearing only a t-shirt and shorts, I identified myself as a police officer. A woman who I think was a nurse told me the victim was dead. I made sure someone had called 911 and asked the witnesses to stick around. The other motorcyclist was a big man and he kept trying to go to his friend. I had to hold him back and it got a little tense. He was absolutely distraught and very emotional. Death and sudden injury is such a remote possibility to some young people, so when it happens it can be almost incomprehensible. I could hear the sirens of the approaching emergency vehicles and was relieved.

When the first officers arrived, I turned the surviving rider over to them. I briefed the officers about what I knew and pointed out witnesses. I wrote a brief statement and then ran home. My wife wondered where I had been. I told her what had happened and then tried to put the incident in the place where you put those things when you are a police officer.

A lot of things I did and experienced over the course of my policing career affected my family and children, though never directly, until one day when I stopped to get gas at a service station owned by a local First Nation. You get a small discount on your gas if you are a status Indian and, with having four small children, every penny counted. I was inside paying for the gas when I saw a man approaching. I had arrested his uncle, an extremely violent man, several times and he was currently in jail. The man looked wild and very intent on confrontation. He was yelling that I had betrayed my own people and I knew I was probably going to have to fight. The gas station staff blocked him and pushed him out the door. He was still yelling and swearing. I wanted to get back to my van because my wife and children had witnessed this. I thanked the staff, but I was seething with anger. I had always tried to keep my work away from my home life. The man hadn't done anything he could be charged for, so I chalked it up as a regrettable incident and carried on.

A couple of years later I got my first cellphone. I had been a little slow out of the gate, being averse to the idea that people could get a hold of me whenever they wanted to. One day my wife, children, and I were leaving a grocery store when I saw a young offender who was unlawfully at large from a youth detention facility. He was part of an up-and-coming street gang and was very dangerous. I called 911 and asked for officers to come and arrest him. I told communications I would direct officers to the suspect. My wife and kids knew we were just going to watch this guy. He went into a restaurant with three exits, so we positioned ourselves to cover the two most likely ones he would come out of. My oldest son volunteered to cover the one exit we couldn't see. I remember my wife and I saying no at the same time.

I didn't think the young offender would have suspected that the occupants of a big red van with a couple of car seats were watching him. After a few tense moments, a patrol car arrived and shortly after the suspect was in custody. I had broken my own rule about doing police work when my family was with me. But the cellphone had given me distance, and the offender was definitely a high-priority arrest, so I did it. After getting out, the young offender turned eighteen and eventually stabbed a man during a robbery. He received a five-year sentence and fell off the radar afterwards.

In the latter part of my career, off-duty incidents began to increase in frequency. One time I finished a day shift and called home to see if we needed anything. My wife asked me to stop and get a bottle of wine for the evening. I got to the store and, as I was walking in the door, one of the staff pointed to a man getting in a pickup truck. The staff member told me the driver had been refused service and was "just pissed drunk." The employee knew I was a police officer so, like it or not, I felt the pressure and a moral obligation to act.

The driver was a middle-aged man, and I could smell the alcohol on him as soon as I opened his driver's door. He was drunk. This is where lawyers make the most out of technicalities in impaired driving cases. There is a gray area between the formulation of the grounds to make the arrest and the need for action to prevent a drunk driver from driving off. I reached in and shut off the truck. I removed the keys and told him I was a police officer. I kept him in his vehicle and called 911. He was getting agitated and, in spite of knowing he wasn't free to go, insisted he would just leave the vehicle.

A couple of young men, not knowing what was going on, started to approach, telling me to leave the old guy alone. I had my hands full, so I pulled back my coat and showed them my gun and said I was a police officer. They gave each other a quick look and then walked away. Patrol members arrived and took custody of the driver. I arrived home, late as usual.

Another off-duty incident occurred on a bitterly cold December evening when my wife and I were headed to our platoon Christmas party. As we pulled onto the freeway, we saw an older vehicle speeding in the same direction we were going, straddling two lanes. The vehicle then slowed down to twenty kilometres and then sped up again. My wife was driving, so I told her to stay back. The driver almost hit another vehicle and a guardrail. I called 911 and we continued to follow the obviously drunk driver. The 911 operator kept asking for updates as we approached the downtown. I was very fearful this driver would kill or injure an innocent person. The driver eventually reached the city centre and turned onto a surface street. A patrol car finally caught up with us and stopped the vehicle.

I recognized the driver as a man I had arrested several times before. He had a partially consumed bottle of vodka on the front seat beside him. When I got out of my car, the combination of adrenaline and thin dress pants in the Saskatchewan winter had me shivering like a wet dog. I gave information to the officer, so he could formulate the grounds to arrest the driver, and off we went to our Christmas party. My wife was pretty animated, and we had a story to tell. Incidents like this take their toll when you're not working, and they seemed to be happening more often when, at that stage of my career, I wanted them to happen less. I didn't want to make my wife a witness to a tragedy if the driver had careened into someone. The possibilities were end-less and not very many were good. We got lucky.

During that same time period, gang members handling a firearm shot a child in the head. The gun discharged and the bullet went through a wall, striking the child. I was off duty when the incident occurred, and officers quickly identified those responsible. I worked my shift without locating the one outstanding suspect. Once off duty, I went to a local mall to get something and I spotted the suspect by the movie theatre. The location was a dead zone for cellphones. I didn't know if the suspect was armed. There were way too many people around to confront him. My heart was pounding because of the nature of the accusation and the fact the victim was a child. At the last minute, the suspect spotted me and ran out of the mall into a transit bus pickup area. I lost sight of him and he was gone. But we knew he was in the city and, eventually out of options, he turned himself in to the police.

This encounter really made me think about how far I would go to arrest someone when I wasn't working, and whether I wanted this responsibility anymore. I was getting close to being able to retire from policing and try something less stressful. I think I knew this inner conflict would eventually come to a head.

On Good Friday, in 2013, my wife wanted to take me to Costco. I hate shopping at the best of times and I told her I wanted a coffee before we went there. We stopped at a local McDonald's, which was part of a busy mall. When we finally found a place to park, I heard a couple yelling at each other from separate vehicles. They were parked in the same row as us and just a couple vehicles over. They were yelling at each other in a language I didn't understand. They were both very animated and angry. I turned to my wife to bring her attention to them. When I turned back, the man was out of his vehicle and punching the woman through the window of her car. I told my wife to call 911 and jumped out to stop him.

In the time it took me to get past two parked vehicles he punched her at least four times. I announced myself as police and told him to step away from her. He turned and looked at me with a defiant look of "How dare you try to stop me?" I told him to show me his hands. His right hand was behind the woman's head and still inside the vehicle. I didn't know if he had a weapon or not. I pulled my gun and ordered him to step back. He did, and the woman immediately got out of her car and started yelling at me.

"It's my fault. I insulted him, I followed him and insulted him!" she shouted. She got between the man and me, so I holstered my gun. When she realized I was a policeman, she began to scream at me, "Who are you to interfere with us? You can't tell us how to live!"

Other people had seen this incident and had also called 911, but most of them were calling in regard to a man with a gun. The man was uncooperative and kept moving away from me. The woman was trying to run interference. I touched him on the chest and told him he was under arrest for assault. He tried to leave, but I pulled the keys out of his vehicle. We had a bit of a standoff, but I could hear sirens and knew the police were coming.

At this stage of my career, there were a lot of new officers and I wasn't a hundred percent sure the officers coming would recognize me on sight. After what seemed a long period of time, a patrol car arrived. A young constable who I knew on sight but had never worked with got out of his vehicle. I got his cuffs and handcuffed the male. I advised him of his rights a couple times, and now he had to stand still and listen. He refused to acknowledge them. The woman wanted my badge number and said she would be making a complaint. She told the officers who had come as backup that she loved the arrested male and would die for him.

While all of this was going on, my wife was on the phone to 911. It upset me that she had to see me in work mode. My wife went and spoke with an elderly woman who had watched the whole thing and had been frozen in place until the uniformed police arrived. My wife told her I was police officer. The woman thought I was robbing the couple. After the arrested man was transported to the station, I told the constables I would come in and leave my report after I went to Costco.

Sure enough, we still went shopping. We talked about the incident and I apologized for disrupting our day. I had an extra shot of adrenaline because my wife was with me when this happened, and it took a bit of work to dump it. She did a good job watching my back and communicating what was going on to the dispatchers. Perception is everything when an incident like this happens. In a crowded mall parking lot, everybody was just catching bits, but the man with the gun definitely gets the most attention.

I carried my gun off duty for years because of all the threats I received. This incident was the first time I ever drew it. I had rated the threat level posed by this man as very high. He was unknown to me, and he was punching a woman in the face through the window of her car in broad daylight in a crowded parking lot. Who knew what he was capable of doing? He obviously had no fear of the consequences. But violence against women is unacceptable and there has to be consequences. I don't know what happened in court. I never received a court notice, so it was resolved one way or the other.

I moved on from policing six months later. I'd had enough.

As our country grows and the expectations of what we want from the police grow, there will have to be clearly defined rules for police in situations like the ones I have described. It has been ad hoc for much too long, and I wish I were able to help formulate the policies.

In this age of terrorism, school shootings, and criminals who commit brazen acts without seeming to fear the outcome, we need to have police officers ready and able to react, whether they are working or not. This wouldn't be for every officer, so identifying the ones who, by virtue of their willingness and tested skills, are willing to step up when something happens is important. Doing this would enhance the capabilities of police services. Those officers would also have to know they have the support of their administrations and citizens. Crime and violence does not always wait until you are on duty.

CHAPTER 11
POLICING AND PAYING THE ULTIMATE PRICE

As an ex-police officer who has seen the results of violence and killing too many times, I still follow the news in spite of myself. Whenever the police shoot someone, and whenever a police officer is shot, the first question I have is what happened? The second question is why did it happen?

The first question gets answered quickly from many sources. The second takes time, and I do my best not to comment until I have some idea as to the answer. In July 2016, the morning after fourteen police officers in Dallas, Texas, were shot—five killed and nine wounded—I received messages from reporters in Saskatoon, asking me for my comments. I declined because I didn't want to add my voice to the hundreds of people already expressing their points of view from their own perspectives on a tragedy we knew so little about. As an ex-police officer, I personally felt the frustration and pain I suspect all police officers felt. It's like being kicked in the stomach and trying to catch your breath when you see fellow police officers murdered for doing their jobs. The day after the shootings was a lost day.

People commenting on tragic events often say they can't imagine the pain everyone is feeling. I can and do understand the enormity of tragedies like this.

Within ten days, six more officers were shot in Baton Rouge, Louisiana—three dead and three wounded. Twenty families devastated in ten days, and thousands of police officers across North America still went to work and carried on. You have to wonder how anyone in law enforcement south of the border could go to work after such carnage. But they did and have been on duty around the clock as they always are.

It's the same for officers in Canada. They report in and head off to do their jobs as always. They do it because they have a sense of duty and obligation. They have sworn an oath to protect. They are still going to take the calls. The reality of everyday policing is you still have to do your job in spite of everything else going on in the world. You have to refocus and stay on your game. The missing child, the victim of domestic violence, and the thousands of other situations still have to be dealt with.

The murder of police officers in Canada is still a very significant event because our population is one-tenth that of the United States. In the United States a single officer who is killed in the line of duty remains a local story if there isn't a titillating circumstance to make it newsworthy to the rest of the country. News sources want stories and, except for local interest, murders have become all too common place unless there is special significance. When the police shoot someone, it's always newsworthy, and the why is often lost in the next wave of news. Long after most people have made their own conclusions and judgments, the results of an investigation are released to a page three paragraph, if reported at all. From my own observations and experience, the police use force when they fear for their safety or the safety of the public. Whether or not their fear is justified is put under intense scrutiny through the media, courts, and public opinion, even more so now with social media and video.

Fear is a powerful influence when you are dealing with an unknown subject during a police contact. Undoubtedly, it has led to overreaction by some police officers, leading to the deaths of civilians, or an underreaction, leading to the deaths of police officers. Eliminating the fear of the unknown is a near impossibility, but police committed to one community and seeing the residents as their own is a good starting point. Fear and hate flourish when we don't know each other.

The killing of four RCMP officers in Mayerthorpe, Alberta; three in Moncton, New Brunswick; two in Spiritwood, Saskatchewan, and most of the other murders of police officers have been committed by people who have a deep-seated hatred for the police and what the police stand for. The killers believe they have a grievance against the police that justifies their actions. This is not a new thing. In the early eighties, two young men who had the intention to murder a police officer when they left their homes that day murdered an officer in Saskatoon. Hatred for the police, for whatever reason, is a reality for some people.

On the other side of things, I have seen many of the videos showing police in the United States shooting and killing people. In some of them, the actions of the officers were cowardly and criminal and they were dealt with accordingly. In many others, a thirty-second clip did nothing to help me understand the shooting, other than showing that someone had been shot. After watching these videos, I try to read up on the case to see what had transpired up until and after the shooting. Like with every incident involving the police, there is an investigation. An investigation where the stakes are high and there is a post-case examination to prevent or mitigate the chances of a similar tragic outcome.

Some people, though, express outrage without knowledge and simply provide kindling for what I'll call the fires of hatred, which just raises the chances of more carnage down the road. There are cowards and racists in every segment of our society. Petty people who, once they are given authority, become cruel and inflexible. We pay for incompetent and bad people in all walks of life every day, one way or another. But we do not advocate disbanding the legal profession or a police force for the odd bad actor. We deal with the bad ones one at a time, just like we should with every incident involving a questionable police shooting.

As an ex-police officer, I have very high expectations of serving officers. I expect them to be professional and bias-free. Having dealt with thousands of different people, I know perfection is unattainable and there will always be those who have faults. Those faults have to be discovered and weeded out. Meanwhile, the vast majority of the police officers in Canada continue to serve faithfully and well, even if it means sacrificing their own lives.

When the RCMP officers were murdered in Mayerthorpe in March 2005, I was on holidays. A large contingent of officers from the Saskatoon Police went to the funerals and services. I had returned to work and was on duty, so I couldn't go.

I've avoided funerals for most of my adult life. Perhaps by going to one, I felt I was highlighting my own mortality, or perhaps I had used up so much emotion in my everyday life, especially after I'd started policing, that I didn't have a lot to give anymore. I knew at some point, like everyone else, I would be called upon to attend a funeral, life being what it is. You must show support for others in their hour of grief. When it came to police funerals, I thought if I didn't go I was somehow protecting myself. Raw grief is like an exposed nerve, and I found it so hard to deal with on a personal level.

I was finally backed into a corner when a young patrolman with the Saskatoon Police Service died of leukemia shortly after I started. He graduated a couple classes behind me. I didn't know him personally. Very early in his career he fell ill and died a remarkably short time afterwards. His first signs of illness came while he was on duty. A quick diagnosis, followed by a short period of treatment, and he was gone. His death struck his classmates from police college hard. I was off duty when his funeral was held, and I had no excuse not to go.

The outpouring of emotion at his service was overwhelming, his family and classmates from police college humbled me. My first police funeral and I was as much of a coward as I had ever been. It felt as if I acknowledged grief and death, I made us all more vulnerable to it.

Officers were being killed or dying across Canada throughout my career after that first funeral. I always seemed to find a reason or excuse not to go to the funerals. I was on duty, or I had court—anything, as long as I didn't have to go. I was doing a good job of avoiding police funerals until April 2006.

That was when a young constable died of unknown or undetermined causes after a day of training with the public order unit. At the end of the training day, he went home and died during the night. It was an absolute thunderbolt to everyone, especially to the members of his platoon. He was a natural leader, popular and easygoing. I had just been assigned to his shift as an acting sergeant until my promotion was confirmed. As a leader, I had no place to hide. I attended the funeral and was hardly able to breath. The collective grief of his family, his platoon, and the entire service was undeniable. I could barely march. I did not cry. I thought it was important as a leader not to. The job would be waiting. It always was and will be. Patrol members were still taking calls during the funeral.

I very rarely shed a tear throughout my service. A murder of a mother in front of her children, the death of a twelve-year-old by hanging, and the deaths of a wife and husband in the aftermath of a police chase broke the dams for me, but only for a moment. Then I went back to being the "tough guy." In retrospect, my own and many other police officers' failure to grieve probably contributes to post-traumatic stress. You can only hold back so much.

Less than three months after my second police funeral, two RCMP members were murdered in Saskatchewan. I went to the funeral of one of the officers in Regina at the RCMP Depot. I was on duty for the second funeral. After nineteen years of service, I was finally stepping up and sharing in the collective grief of my comrades.

In June 2011, a young offender murdered a constable with the York Regional Police with a vehicle. I was selected by our police association to attend the funeral with two other members of our service. There were thousands of officers there from all over North America. The procession was the biggest I had ever been a part of. It was the most fitting way I could imagine to honour this officer.

I have been to four police funerals in total: two officers died at the hands of criminals; one died of leukemia; one of unknown causes. As I mentioned earlier, many other officers were killed or died over the course of my career, but the nature of shift work, the distance, costs of travel, and the need to have officers on the streets during the funerals kept me from attending (or, rather, allowed me not to attend). As it was, four funerals were enough for me.

All of the funerals were very public and well attended by uniformed police officers. For the most part, officers have been supportive and respectful of the various services as they

buried one of their members. They will always be remembered as family, a brother or sister to the mourners—such is
the nature of police work. Amidst the grief and uncertainty of
these deaths, there were people who questioned or derided the
size and scope of the funerals. They cited costs and whatever
else they could think of to question the value of public displays
of grief.

Police officers know only too well the gap left by the sudden
deaths of people in our communities. We understand the pain
of the survivors and everyone affected by death. We notify families and try to help them understand what happened. When
it's one of our own, it's even harder because we often know the
details most other families are spared. There are not a lot of
professions left where a condition of employment includes the
swearing of a solemn oath. In policing, the oaths almost always
include the words "protect" and "serve."

Police funerals are an acknowledgement of the risks we as
police officers take every day. I have stood with thousands of
other officers and marched in the funeral processions, even
though I never knew two of the officers whose funerals I
attended. Why? Because I knew what they did and what they
stood for. At every funeral, every procession, I was in a sea
of people, each alone with their thoughts. It was necessary to
show and feel the support of the other police officers and their
communities so I could keep going back out on the streets year
after year. I'm pretty certain other officers felt the same way.

There are many different attendees at police funerals. The
media often attend police funerals because of their high profile
and, from my experience, generally cover them in a respectful
manner. The critics are always free to watch or not watch, and
they tend to treat police funerals like any other funeral happening in their communities. For the families of the officers who

have been killed or who have died, though, nothing will ever be the same.

Meanwhile, the extended family of the dead—their fellow police officers—still have to dry their tears, put away their dress uniforms, and then head back out onto the street and carry on with their duties. The police funerals they attend give them a chance to say goodbye before placing themselves in harm's way once again.

CHAPTER 12
THE MEDIA AND THE POLICE

I have had a great relationship with the media over the years. I have been fortunate in that I've met many dedicated and committed reporters. As a serving officer, and now as a retired police officer turned writer, this relationship has remained strong. I'm very grateful for the many times I have been asked for and have given my opinion on some difficult issues. I have had the opportunity to speak to thousands of people through the media and through public speaking.

The audiences have been very diverse. I have talked to bankers, teachers, health care professionals, and police officers. I have talked at schools, from primary level to universities. Indigenous organizations, from band councils to the Saskatchewan Indian Gaming Authority, have asked me to speak at conferences and gatherings. By far, most people have been very receptive and, while a little stressful, most of the talks have been enjoyable experiences for me. Being given the chance to talk about my experiences with leadership, self-reliance, First Nations, policing, as well as being given an opportunity to offer a different perspective, has been very rewarding for me.

When I first started policing in Saskatoon, I received more attention from the media than I wanted or felt I deserved. I understand it now, thirty years later. The third Indigenous officer for the Saskatoon Police Service after its many years of existence was a story I would have covered if I were a reporter back in 1987.

I think at many levels my hiring showed the winds of change were blowing for the Saskatoon Police. I assumed that, like with many other news stories, my story would be forgotten fairly quickly. But in the First Nations community it was not forgotten, and I was regularly told there were high expectations now that I was out on the streets.

After some of the incidents with the military police, I was cautious when people tried to tie their agendas to what I was doing. Most people were genuine and sincere when offering me opportunities to engage with the community and some were not. As a trained soldier and police officer, I was prepared to avoid ambushes in the most stressful life and death situations. But nothing prepared me for my first real experience with a media ambush interview.

It happened in the early '90s. I don't know exactly how it came about, as I was still a uniformed constable working in patrol. I think the Native Liaison Constable, who normally handled media requests from First Nations agencies, was unable to attend.

I was assigned to go to Winnipeg to be part of a panel the Aboriginal Peoples Television Network (APTN) had put together to talk about in-custody deaths of First Nations people. It was a very emotional topic and I could have declined. But I felt honoured to be included in such an important discussion and felt taking part was part of being a leader in my own community.

The staff at APTN were very helpful to a rookie panelist. The relationship between the police and First Nations, especially municipal police officers in the prairies, had seen some difficult times in the eighties and early nineties. So I wasn't sure what the reception would be like. I was in the APTN studio—this was their house.

When the time for the show came, I was ready for a possibly heated discussion of a very important topic for all of us. The show opened with a short documentary that, in my opinion, lacked balance and was definitively slanted against the police. Statements made by individuals appearing in the documentary were taken as facts and presented without context or counter-arguments. Background information, which would have provided context, was left out, and the viewers were left to feel there was no other reasonable conclusion available other than the documentary maker's conclusion, namely, that the police were abusing and causing the deaths of First Nations people while they were in custody.

My true position as an invited panelist became very readily apparent. It seemed as if people were going to get free rein to make accusations and inflame viewers. I realized I was sitting on a kind of powder keg and the documentary had lit the fuse. Here I was on a national television program in front of many of my own friends, relations, colleagues, and bosses, along with a significant TV audience, many of whom had real and some perceived grievances against police officers.

I weighed my words very carefully when pointing out that the entire story had not been presented. I stated I had more questions than answers after watching the film. After watching the documentary, the average person watching at home may have felt that First Nations people routinely died in police custody and that the police routinely covered it up.

Referring to my own experience, I pointed out this was simply not the case. In-custody deaths are relatively rare in Canada, I explained. Every "in-custody" death is subject to an intensive investigation by the police, media, government agencies, and the coroner's office. There is always a coroner's inquest. It is the law, I told my interviewer. People who die in police custody, or during the course of an arrest, die for many reasons, some of them totally out of the control of the police. For example, some people have pre-existing medical conditions that are exacerbated by drug and alcohol consumption. A fight with police while resisting arrest, coupled with those factors, sometimes also contributes to unfortunate deaths. If there had been a criminal act by the police, they would have been held accountable, I said.

I applied my experience to the panel and fielded calls from viewers. It was my first experience on a panel where I was clearly on the unpopular side. I was tired when my interview was over and a bit wiser. I think I brought some balance to an emotional discussion when all was said and done.

I became an ardent supporter of balance when it came to reporting stories about the police in the early nineties. A story broke about ritual satanic sexual abuse in Saskatchewan, allegedly involving members of the Saskatoon Police. I was a fairly junior constable in uniform at the time, so I wasn't privy to the details of the investigation. So all I had to form my own opinion on the Martensville Scandal, as it came to be called, were rumours swirling around the station. I began to have doubts about some members of the service. In other words, I had bought into the scandal without balance.

Inexperience and some immaturity on my part caused me the private embarrassment I have always regretted after taking the hook, line, and sinker of a story without any critical examination. As it was, the alleged offences were proven to be deeply flawed and the allegations unfounded. In the aftermath, the damage to the publicly named officers was substantial and long lasting. I almost got swept up in the hysteria about cults, which started in the United States and found its way to Saskatchewan—the "Satanic Panic" as some called it in the media back then.

This was all twenty-five or more years ago when the news sources were limited to television, print, and radio. Any balance in the presentation of news stories concerning the police depended on the relationship the police had with the media organization—and sometimes that was precarious.

Police officers who commit criminal acts, or who are incompetent, are the bane of thousands of police officers that do their duty in good faith every day. The tendency to paint police officers with a broad brush every time an incident of police misconduct arises has not lost any momentum over time. If anything, the internet has brought out both the worst and best of reporting on police-related stories. Fairness and objectivity in stories about the police were and are the first casualties with online sources of information. People can post any stories they want online with little to no consequence, as they aren't accountable to any media standards oversight organization. The traditional media, meanwhile, has been struggling to survive financially in this new reality. This has had it sometimes joining in with these sensationalists to retain its audience.

The police officers I worked with just wanted the media to be fair and impartial. Indigenous people understand this as well as anyone. There has been a push in the past couple of years to address disparities in the coverage of Indigenous issues. Forward-thinking Indigenous journalists have been pointing out the effects of repeated negative coverage of First Nations issues by the mainstream media and, slowly, it has been changing.

There will always be struggles and challenges for all Canadians that will reflect poorly on all of us. If stories are reported fairly and in context, we will not inflame and enrage people against any particular group or organization. I have belonged, and continue to belong, to three distinct groups that suffer as a result of sweeping judgments and assumptions made by people who are only getting half the story: Indigenous people, soldiers, and police officers.

In October 2015, I was in northern Ontario for the moose hunt when I was contacted through my publisher and asked if I would take part in a radio discussion. The subject matter was whether or not police should investigate other officers when allegations of criminal conduct have been made against them. The catalyst for the story was the then breaking allegations of sexual abuse of Indigenous women by Quebec provincial police members in northern Quebec.

Even though I was out hunting, I had been following the story because the allegations were so serious. The story's implications were so potentially explosive to the relations between police and Indigenous people—not only in Quebec but across the country—that I thought I could provide some perspective based on my experiences. I agreed to take the phone call and be part of the conversation. The other person involved was an Indigenous woman. She was a well-known activist and lawyer.

The radio show started by reciting the chronology of the story and how events had unfolded up to the date of the show. The host wasted no time in getting to the topic of police investigating other police, and he put me on the chopping block first. (It felt weird sitting in my parents' cabin in northern Ontario, talking on a national broadcast radio show.)

To start off, I stated I thought the police assigned to investigate the allegations would do a thorough job because there was so much at stake. Police need the confidence of all communities to do their jobs and protect the community. Every allegation of misconduct or criminal wrongdoing, I added, reflects on all fifty thousand police officers in the country. The nature and scope of an investigation like this requires experience-acquired expertise. Police have the resources and knowledge required to conduct the investigation and are accountable for the outcome.

I also reflected on my experience when the RCMP were investigating the Saskatoon Police in the wake of the "Starlight Tours" allegations in the period of 2000 to 2005. The RCMP officers did their jobs investigating the alleged mistreatment of a young Indigenous man, Neil Stonechild, who was found frozen to death one cold winter's night in a field just outside Saskatoon. Police colleagues of mine paid with their jobs and were prosecuted in connection with the case. There was no favouritism or sense of brotherhood shown by the RCMP during the investigation, I said. The Mounties were after the truth and the facts.

Then the host put the question to the other guest.

She would have none of it. At an emotional, fast-paced clip, in the course of the thirteen-minute discussion, she quoted research, inquiry reports, and other sources to stake out her position. She called the entire Quebec provincial police force thugs. She used words like "rampant" and "pervasive," and alleged there were thousands of incidents involving the police across Canada.

She then laced into the RCMP and alleged they regularly committed gang rapes. She laid waste to my suggestion the Saskatchewan police have made great progress in improving relations with the Indigenous community. Lastly, her position on the high rate of victimization of Indigenous women was to lay the blame clearly at the feet of the police.

During her interview, she made some pretty fiery and inflammatory statements about the police that weren't grounded in the facts. Clearly, she was being more of an activist and less of a lawyer committed to the facts during the course of our conversation. I thought what she said was a disservice to the thousands of men and women faithfully serving and protecting their communities as police officers. Granted, to deny there are some police officers who are racist, or that some police officers commit crimes, is equally unrealistic. But the vast majority of police do their jobs with honour and distinction every day, no matter what stories, accusations, or misrepresentations are out there. When I hung up the phone, I commented to my mother, "We are very blessed to live in a free country."

Indigenous people have had many reasons in the past to be suspicious of police-led investigations of other police in Canada. But I believe the new realities of 24/7 media and the strong voices of Indigenous leaders have made it very difficult to cover up or downplay allegations of misconduct. Politicians are part of the equation now, as well, and the good ones want to be seen as advocates for social justice. Even that surreal interview on the phone in my parents' cabin in northern Ontario plays a part in the new dialogues taking place every day. Being loud or using divisive language doesn't make you right, but it doesn't make you wrong either.

As the keeper of the keys, when incidents involving police or affecting the community they serve occur, police services have an important duty to release information to the media through media releases. I remember doing media releases when I was working as an acting staff sergeant. Media releases contain the information the police release to the media to keep the public informed. After an incident had occurred, and after gathering as much information as was possible from officers at the scene, I would type out a release and disseminate it through the police website. Often, as the incident was unfolding or concluding,

I had to race to get the information out before the media called me. The media would call frequently, looking for updates, even as I was trying to get a clear picture of what was going on myself. For very high-profile events like disasters or murders, the media relations officer would come in and handle all media inquiries. However, the reality was most of the time you were on your own handling inquiries and doing press releases.

It's funny, now that I'm no longer policing, to realize I had no training at all for the role of releasing information to the media. There were times when dealing with reporters was stressful because they had a duty to report events in a timely matter. On my end, I had a duty not to jeopardize police work by revealing information during ongoing incidents and investigations. Overall, I found if you were as forthcoming and honest as you could be with reporters, they respected the boundaries. The relationship doesn't have to be adversarial between police and media.

There was a time when I first started when relations were anything but friendly. We were told never to talk to reporters. We were constantly warned to watch what we said because it could have been twisted to put the police in a bad light. We were told reporters would sit behind officers having lunch or coffee in restaurants just to overhear our conversations. But I didn't understand the paranoia of senior officers in regard to the media. It seemed to normalize for a while in the 1990s. However, in the 2000s, in Saskatoon, when the scandals and inquiries started in regard to the so-called Starlight Tours I mentioned earlier, it was back and stronger than ever.

As a serving police officer, and now as a citizen, I have had a great personal relationship with the media. I see the people in the media as leaders. That being said, not all leaders are as good or as competent as they should be in any trade, including the media. They are leaders just the same. Members of the media have the means to inform, influence, and provide leadership to all Canadians.

The police and the media have both undergone major changes in the past twenty years. Some changes, like improved technology and higher levels of education for entrants into their respective trades, are to be expected with the affluence we have enjoyed. Other changes, though, like the loss of experience through retirement, came unexpectedly to both fields. Maybe the demographics of our population made it unavoidable, but there has been a loss of experienced people in both fields. And that can lead to friction between the media and police.

Younger reporters are less expensive to hire and, wanting to make a name for themselves, they are more cost-effective. We have been fortunate that a lot of these young people have stepped up and done well, at least in Canada. Yet there have been times when, as a middle-aged man who has to wait for the news like everyone else now, I cringe at a young reporter's choice of words.

Reporting on police and crime is at best difficult. The reporter's own values and life experience can affect the report. If the editor has similar beliefs and values, the report can have a direct effect on how the news is received in the community. How the community reacts to the news and the police can sometimes be influenced by those reports. There are many examples from the United States where reports of police-involved shootings, never tried in the courts, have led directly to violence against the police.

Since leaving policing, I have had the opportunity to speak to a group of people from the media. The lead editor from a local news station invited me to provide an informal workshop on how reporters and news crews could more effectively report on police and First Nations stories. I talked about leadership by the media and the importance of what they do. A lot of people in all sorts of different professions don't see themselves as leaders and seem surprised when I tell them they are.

There were a lot of questions. The questions reflected the experiences of the people asking them. Some were very specific, like how to cover a crime or violent incident if the news team arrives before the police do. I actually believe this will happen more and more as our cities grow—the police will not always be the first to arrive.

At the workshop I emphasized personal safety first and cautioned news teams not to become part of the story, unless they are rescuing someone in noncriminal distress. I talked about how important it is not to canvass witnesses at a major crime scene. Canvassing witnesses before investigators even begin their work and using the material in a broadcast can be problematic when the witness's version changes in court. It could also land media people in court. And I've spent enough time in court to know it's better not to be there.

A caveat to my advice is if you are a photographer or cameraman at a scene, snap or shoot away, if you can do so safely. I remember one case in the 1990s where a woman was stabbed in the stomach outside of the Barry Hotel, a formerly notorious establishment now demolished and turned into a parking lot in Saskatoon. A news photographer caught an image of the woman holding her wound with blood soaking her jeans. The expression of pain and surprise on her face was very powerful. It appeared on the front page of the paper and sparked an outcry that led the Saskatoon Police to make a concerted effort to try and reduce the crime rate in the area by increasing the manpower assigned there. It took a picture to get something going because it seemed there had been an indifference to the violence up to that point.

Ultimately, the relationship between the police and mainstream media boils down to trust in each other to do what's right for the right reasons. The leadership from both groups can affect a community's sense of well-being and security. The media needs to be separate and impartial as it seeks the truth, while being mindful of its leadership responsibilities. Citizens are well served if they are well informed.

CHAPTER 13
DEALING WITH PTSD

I have just started my third year as a civilian. I have written previously in my first two books about post-traumatic stress and how it affected not only me but also my family. Even after admitting the job had taken a toll on me, my wife Christine said I wasn't done writing or talking about it. I stubbornly argued that I was finished, and that I was getting better with it every day. We were both right, I believe. I *am* getting better at dealing with what I have seen and experienced. Time, as almost every senior citizen has told me over my lifetime, has a way of healing you. My wife was also right—I am not done writing about it.

You never really walk away from experiences you have as a first responder. In the past three years, there have been many stories in the news about first responders and the price they pay doing their jobs in an increasingly complex and often violent world. Some, unfortunately, have been unable to cope and have taken their own lives. Every time I read a story about a first responder suicide, I can't help but wonder how it came to such a desperate end.

Post-traumatic stress and post-traumatic stress disorder (PTSD) have been around in some form or another from the time people were able to think and experience trauma. A person suffering from what we now call post-traumatic stress could be described as being in shock, the cat having taken their tongue, having seen the ghost, or any other descriptor used to convey extreme reaction to trauma.

Many viewed post-traumatic stress with suspicion, fearing it and considering it unmanly. People suffering from post-traumatic stress would be called hysterical, high-strung, and touched. The effects of trauma on soldiers raised awareness slowly after the First World War. But even before the Great War, there were attempts to describe soldiers suffering from post-traumatic stress. In the American Civil War, soldiers suffering from post-traumatic stress were said to have "seen the elephant." Soldiers were described as shattered, broken, unbalanced, and not right in the head when they displayed physical and mental signs of post-traumatic stress.

"Shell-shocked" was the first term to really enter into the public conscience during and after the First World War. However, all the old phrases still applied. The harshest words used to describe people suffering from post-traumatic stress were usually handed out by those who feared it the most. They feared it because they didn't understand it or were afraid because they could be next.

During the Second World War, terms like "battle fatigue" entered our language. Because of the high numbers of soldiers involved in both world wars who became mental health casualties, the effects of trauma were studied more than they ever had been in modern history. The more enlightened psychiatrists and forward-thinking doctors looked for a quick cure so they could feed the soldiers back into combat as quickly as possible. Harsh terms were still being used to describe soldiers who had reached their own trauma capacity. Officers trying to cajole men back into the fight used words like "basket case," "shell," and "coward."

I often wonder how so many veterans were able to return to society and function after their experiences of war. One of the most common descriptions of how they coped was what I heard while growing up: "Uncle such-and-such was in the war, but he never talks about it." When I was a boy, there was a German army veteran who drank in the local bar almost every day. He would cry and sing German songs when he was drunk. A loud bang and he would overturn his table and shoot back with an imaginary rifle. One of the boys in town tested the story he had heard and with the cruelty of youth confirmed a loud bang returned the troubled soul to the battlefields. While I was growing up there were still a lot of veterans around. I respected them and didn't ask them about the Second World War or Korea, having been told, "They never talk about the war."

I think those words were the start of my initial conditioning to dealing with post- traumatic stress. In the 1970s, Hollywood brought us the damaged Vietnam veterans, either as dark brooding anti-heroes or characters scarred by their experiences trying to fit back into American society. Either way, the conversation about post-traumatic stress was being brought back to the rest of us again. There were a lot of movies that provided superficial looks at the effects of trauma on people in emergency services. Crazy paramedics, burnt-out cops, and hard-living firefighters doing wild and outlandish things because of what they had experienced and seen became serious or humorous entertainment for the rest of us. The mixed messages were there for young men and women entering the military, emergency, and first response fields in real life.

People suffering from, affected by, or dealing with post-traumatic stress disorder are in all segments of our society.

Many communities in Canada have had tragedies that, afterward, have left people with all the symptoms and the struggles. The school shooting in La Loche, Saskatchewan, in January 2016 left four dead and seven physically wounded and left many others dealing with post-incident trauma. The train derailment and fire in July 2013 at Lac-Mégantic, Quebec, left forty-two dead, five people missing and presumed dead, and forever changed the residents there.

Even in communities affected by shared tragedy, the response to the trauma by each person will be as individual as they are. Victims of violent crimes like sexual abuse, domestic assaults, and robberies all suffer and also have to deal with the aftermath. Family members of homicide victims and the victims of drunk drivers all have to deal with post-traumatic stress. Some people are unable to stop the trauma experience from turning into a mental health issue.

Certainly, we have made some progress in past years in understanding mental health issues arising from post-traumatic stress in civilians, but many people have slipped back into society untreated, angry, self-medicating, and feeling abandoned. First responders will be the ones dealing with them if they suffer a breakdown, becoming unable to stay within social and legal norms. Many criminals—while it doesn't excuse their crimes—have unresolved trauma issues.

No one told me any of this as I began my journey into a life and career in uniform. I don't think recruiters would do very well if they told potential recruits, "Oh, yes, I almost forgot to mention, you will see things that will shock you to your core, so traumatic you won't be able to sleep, and it will all hang around for many years after you are finished." To tell the truth, most people don't give those things much thought, and even if some did, it probably wouldn't be the recruiters.

Like so many men and women who choose to serve in professions where the helping, protecting, and problem-solving aspects of your job involve other human beings, I came into policing believing I was ready for anything. Not every first responder is suffering with post-trauma stress. Every person has a finite capacity for trauma. Some first responders make it through their entire career before the traumas catch up with them. Some have remarkable coping skills or support systems that help them move through their careers. Building capacity to deal with trauma is a leadership skill. Leaders in all point-of-contact emergency services are beginning to realize that the people who help others through traumas need to be healthy as well.

My preconditioning for the career I had chosen was as individual as any other person. My generation was fed a steady diet of mixed messages about what was expected from a man. You had to be tough. You never showed weakness. Things you did and saw shouldn't bother you. At the same time, you had to be inclusive and sensitive to other people's needs.

My personal experiences included exposure to domestic violence at a young age, which included being bullied and beaten up many times when I was young. Watching men fight outside of the local bar was part of the weekend entertainment in a small town before the coming of television. We hunted and killed animals. I was also exposed to racism and cruelty. When you're younger, your capacity to deal with these things is still pretty high, which is why young people recover from trauma faster. We have all heard or said, "They're young. They'll bounce back."

In the late 1990s, I took an injury accident call in front of a school. A six-year-old boy was waiting to cross the street and a van passed by him. He was in a hurry, so as soon as that van passed him, he darted out onto the street. He didn't see the trailer the van was pulling and was struck. He was seriously injured—the corner of the trailer pierced his skull, exposing his brain. The paramedics, firefighters, and I all exchanged glances to acknowledge we didn't think the boy would live. Dealing with the parents afterwards, I felt like I was giving a pre-death notification. Remarkably, I ran into his mother not even two weeks later and she told me her son was out of the hospital. She added he had a long road ahead of him, but he was alive and in good spirits.

Nearly twenty years later, I was asked to speak at a career day at this same school where I had attended this accident. When I parked, I was just metres away from where the boy had been hit. Even after all that time, being in that parking spot brought back the trauma. At least it was a traumatic memory softened, and with a good ending.

But there's more to this story.

In 2017 I was in a northern Saskatchewan community called St. George's Hill doing a speaking engagement. After I was done, I was surprised to be approached by the mother of that boy who was injured in the school accident I remembered so vividly. She thanked me for everything I had done at the call and afterwards. I tried to explain it was a team effort from everyone involved. She then took me to her home and I met her son, now a grown man. It was a very moving experience, and I felt so honoured to have had this unexpected closure to an incident I had never forgotten. I smiled for the whole twelve-hour drive home.

When I joined the army, I joined an organization that actively undertook the role of building trauma capacity in individuals. It started from the moment you got off the bus in basic training and never really stopped until you left. It was especially true for soldiers in the combat arms, in my case, the infantry, whose job it was to inflict trauma on others (but to avoid as much as possible ourselves) if it ever came to war.

In basic training, we were shown films of extremely graphic violent traumas from the '70s, with titles like *Medics in Vietnam* and *Carnage on the Highways.* We even watched a film about childbirth. For most of us eighteen- and nineteen-year-old recruits, who had never seen a child being born, it was a shocker. (I think viewing the intensity of a woman's experience giving birth was the army's way of teaching us not to complain about what we were going to experience.) I don't think any of these productions are too far from what anyone could watch on the internet now. But back then they were shocking to me. Decapitated bodies, soldiers and civilians ripped apart by bullets, bombs, or accidents, with a calm narrator describing the causes, filled the movie screen at my training base.

The desensitizing of soldiers to violence and trauma took many forms. The army breaks down individual values and replaces them with collective ones. If your comrades survive, you will survive. At the same time, the army was trying to build the mental capacity in the recruits to endure the loss of their buddies if it ever came to actual conflict.

During my infantry training, four-fifths of the 125 soldiers that I started with were gone by the end of our course. Many of the recruits who began that training with me became friends during the high-intensity atmosphere of training. But if your new friends were washed out, chances are you would never see them again. You went out for your training day and when you came back their lockers were empty and their mattresses rolled up on their beds. It was like they had never been there.

The injured recruits—"wounded" in army talk—could end up rejoining the unit. But those who quit, or failed, were kept separated from the other recruits. We weren't allowed to talk to them because their lack of will would contaminate us, our

NCOs told us. It was a tough but ingenious way of building capacity to withstand trauma.

The constant theme of creating and maintaining resolve and mental toughness was part of my life almost every day I served. It was in the language and mindset of almost every soldier. We trained with purpose. The purpose was to fight and win if we were called on to do so. Most of my friends from the military were between eighteen and thirty years old. The collective building of capacity to withstand trauma in young men is easier than building it within other groups. So the indoctrination I received from the infantry folded in well when I started with the military police. Not a lot of things shocked me since I'd seen my fair share of violence by then.

There was one incident that did shake me up, though. As a military police officer, I was directly responsible for anyone I arrested. One night I arrested a soldier for impaired driving. He was defiant and resisted arrest. Fortunately, he was drunk enough that I quickly overcame his resistance and in due course he was lodged in a cell. I was working alone that night and after I finished my paper work I headed back out on patrol.

An elderly commissionaire, who answered the phones and called me on the radio if anything needing attention arose, manned the guardhouse. The commissionaire was a man of few words and more than a few times I would catch him taking a quick nap if it was quiet. I was about four kilometres away when his deep voice startled me over the radio. He used the proper radio code, even though I was the only guy working, and said, "MP1, you better come back to the guardhouse—there is something wrong with your prisoner."

I wheeled the patrol car around and raced to the guardhouse. When I arrived, I found my arrested soldier hanging from the bars on the window of his cell. He had used his black nylon dress socks as a noose. I cut him down and told the commissionaire to call the medics. The soldier lived and was taken to the medical orderly room. If the commissionaire had been sleeping, the soldier would have died.

This incident stayed with me a long time. There was no clear policy at the time for the care of prisoners in a situation when you were working alone. The commissionaire was supposed to do periodic cell checks. It was a lot to expect for an eighty-year-old man to stay awake all night and be responsible, at least partly, for a person's life. The soldier was married with children, and, ultimately, if he had died I would have been responsible. I think about this incident whenever I hear about an in-custody death, especially if the death occurs in a small detachment or northern community.

Lessons from traumatic events have to be shared or they become lost lessons benefitting no one. I hadn't even thought of inquiring about the soldier's state of mind, and his suicide attempt was totally unexpected. Inadequate staffing, or staffing positions with undertrained and unqualified people, has led to many tragedies. This incident was very nearly one of them. This is where leadership is so important: clear direction, clarity, and anticipation of worst-case scenarios go a lot further in preventing situations than crossing your fingers and hoping for the best.

The current awareness about the effects of trauma on emergency services and military personnel is a positive step for the rest of us. We need the people who protect and treat us to know we appreciate they do it at a cost to themselves. Just knowing people have empathy for you goes a long way to help and maintain yourself as a first responder.

Some people I have spoken to feel we talk about it too much and that we are creating new cases that might not have existed before. I suppose it's possible that some people might take advantage of the increased awareness of trauma to exploit the benefits that are available, such as they are. I believe these malingerers, though, are in the minority and are, sadly, an unfortunate fact of life. Personal pride and supporting your team aren't always priorities for everyone.

My experiences with the Saskatoon Police Service reflect what is happening in many other Canadian police jurisdictions. As I progressed through my career, I became more experienced, received more training, and was issued better equipment than when I started. The trade-off was I was expected to do more and more every year. The intensity and frequency of calls where I dealt with traumatic events kept increasing year after year. The recovery time between incidents became shorter and shorter. Coupled with an administration and leadership that were trained in the same type of "nothing should bother you" mind-set, all in all, it seemed to be the natural order of things—it was the institutional culture.

And the trauma calls kept coming. On a day shift early in my career, I responded to a call of a baby not breathing. Any call involving injured children gets a very fast lights-and-siren response from all emergency services. A baby not breathing is among the highest priority calls. I arrived first and jumped out of my patrol car, running to the front door. Before I got to the steps, the mother ran out and literally tossed the baby to me. My heart was pumping so hard I was having trouble finding a pulse. You get so focused in these incidents that you can miss a lot of details. I saw but did not hear the ambulance pulling up behind my patrol car. I quickly dashed over and gave the baby to a paramedic.

Only after I did that did I realize the baby's colour was all wrong and that he was probably already dead. The look on the paramedic's face said it all—we will try but don't keep your hopes up. Firefighters, paramedics, and police officers communicate more than they know with expressions only like-minded people would understand. It carries on at the hospitals, as well, with nurses and doctors relaying unspoken communication to give a heads-up to everyone involved in a rescue effort—a kind of across-the-board defence mechanism for people under stress.

I went into the house after the ambulance sped away. I viewed the crib where the baby had been sleeping and looked for anything suspicious. Another officer came and took the mother to the hospital. I received a radio call, advising me with the police numerical code signalling the baby was confirmed dead. Speaking with family members, I was told this was the second SIDS-related (sudden infant death syndrome) death for the mother. This is unusual statistically, so I examined the crib while I was waiting for the sergeant to arrive and take over. The emotion and adrenaline from these calls is intense. As a parent, you never want to consider the possibility something could be amiss in a tragedy like this, but you still have to do your job. Once relieved, I went in and left my report. I spoke to the assigned detective and told him how unusual it was to have two such deaths in one family. I gently suggested he should consider this while conducting his investigation. I never heard anything further.

Unfortunately, this wouldn't be my last infant death, but I learned as I went along what to look for. Some infant deaths were attributed to neglect or callousness, but not enough for the parents to be held criminally responsible. You just carried on. Even after a call like this one, you were expected to take calls immediately afterward. The very next call could be a situation equally as tragic and you were expected to go regardless.

During one shift working as a constable, comprising two twelve-hour days and two twelve-hour nights, I took calls on six sudden deaths—four natural and two suicides. The dispatcher kept apologizing, saying at one point, "I'm so sorry Car 45, but can you take a 45 call again?" using the numerical call sign for a sudden death.

There was no time to process what you saw or experienced at all. You went from call to call. One elderly man had died in his bathroom, and we had to take the door off the hinges to reach him. Another man died of an apparent heart attack in his garage and was found by his son. His face was flat from lying on the concrete for so long. A young man hung himself from the third-floor railing in an apartment building staircase, and his body weight had stretched his neck beyond what you believed was possible.

It was relentless tragedy, but you couldn't call a time out. I thought this is just what policing in a city entails. And, of course, the high-stress traumatic calls were mixed in with all the other more routine calls: the assaults, the robberies, the break-and-enters, all of which had to be attended to. The complainant had no idea where or what you had just come from, so you had to be professional and do your duty.

Here is where the seeds of post-traumatic stress get sown for many first responders. Many of the people in emergency services are driven to help others, driven by a sense of duty compelling them to go from call to call and never complain. Pre-service conditioning and capacity building can only sustain the pace for so long before a person begins to falter. When you throw in the decisions made by leaders—who are so caught up in the politics and economics of putting resources out there to answer calls and, in the process, are forgetting about the people actually handling the emergencies—you are watering the seeds of PTSD.

I began to feel no one other than the people I worked with side-by-side cared how many calls we went to or what we had seen or experienced. Yet I was still both feet on the side of the wire where we didn't talk about our feelings. Many officers working during the eighties and nineties felt the same and had been conditioned the same way. And we were the ones teaching the new officers how to deal with traumatic events.

Saskatoon is and has been ranked among the highest per capita crime rate cities in Canada. The city held its ranking for my entire career. Even if we had wanted to, there wasn't a lot of time to debrief after violent or critical incidents. You just kept going. I don't imagine it was very different in many other police forces across Canada.

I have written about many different critical incidents in my first two books, as well as my physical reaction to them. A big part of the healing process for me has been writing about them. The next step is helping others get through them by sharing what I have learned. When I talk about first responders, I want to ensure I am including everyone because there are many first responders who are consistently not included in conversations about trauma stress.

Police officers, paramedics, and firefighters are usually the first people we include when we talk about emergency first response. Nurses and doctors respond to life and death situations every day as well. Correction officers who guard sentenced prisoners and the sheriffs who transport prisoners and guard them in court deserve special mention because they are charged with the care and protection of people who have a proven disdain for everyone else. They're guarding and caring for people who have committed crimes and are capable of killing or hurting them every minute of every day. There is a lot of stress and much trauma that occurs behind prison walls. To top it off, correction officers and sheriffs are all generally stuck in the same building, working for eight to twelve hours every day.

Through the course of my career, when something horrible or traumatic happened, it was usually at night, when there weren't a lot of people around to see what you had seen. If it happened in the daytime, it was usually in an apartment or house or an isolated location, so it became a personal experience. You could be with five or six other officers, but no one was sharing what we were feeling when we were looking at a twenty-five-year-old man with his head bludgeoned into an indescribable mess. The smell of blood, the smell of bowels released after death—these were not the things you talked about at crime scenes. You knew what you needed to do and you just did it. The conversations never really took place.

How do you talk about crime scenes except in the professional descriptions of trauma required for the purposes of the investigation and, ultimately, the courts? It was not only violent crimes; natural or unnatural deaths that were not criminal still had to be investigated. Investigating a sexual assault where the child was a victim, a domestic assault where a woman was unrecognizable to even her family members, the whole gauntlet of human tragedies—this is where you made your living.

If you couldn't talk about it with the people you worked with, except on a professional level because of the intensity of what you were seeing and experiencing, how could you talk about it when you were done? What do you do when it's time to go home? I think a lot of post-traumatic stress comes from shielding everyone else, especially the ones you love, from what you experience or see. I know for me it was a constant challenge to find balance.

When I came home, I still had to be a husband, father, brother, son, and neighbour. Sometimes I would leave work and think about how I could act so no one knew. How can I hide how I am feeling? Will people know when they look at me that I'm on the edge of losing my composure? When they watch the news, will they ask me if I was there when a horrible story is broadcast? People know when you're a cop or in emergency services, and they are naturally curious when something happens. They aren't being nosy or rude; they just want to know.

All the normal stressors in life, like bills, school, children, and everything else normal life throws at you, almost seem trivial. For the people you love, they are not trivial, because everyday life can be challenging to a person's sense of security and well-being. Yet you can't start a conversation about something important with, "I just came from a teenage suicide, so I don't feel like talking about renewing the mortgage right now." Sharing that isn't fair to anyone else.

Official reviews of what you have done weigh into how you deal with an incident. The reports you file can be read and scrutinized. If it was a public incident, the media will report on it, and members of the public will offer their opinions. If you made mistakes, and even if you didn't, professional standards (our internal affairs department) could review and investigate your actions. In the aftermath of traumatic and critical incidents, the biggest and most influential factor on how you deal with it is ultimately your own values. How did what you had seen and experienced clash with what you believe? What, if any, damage did it do to your beliefs? When you are alone with your thoughts, how do you process the experience?

In the first half of my career, my response was to ask the dispatcher for the next call because that was the way I believed I was coping. When I was off duty, I focused on my family and spent a lot of time with my kids. I ran many kilometres to process, cope, and clear my mind. All of those things helped keep the unprocessed emotions and experiences at bay. However, like any dam built to keep things in place, inevitably something will get through.

All the things I did to keep a handle on my reactions and emotions appeared to work for a long time, until the winter of 1999. I was under more stress than usual then because of an incident a month earlier when a drunk driver in a stolen pickup truck nearly collided with the patrol car I was riding in alongside my partner of six years. The subsequent chase and the arrest of the suspect led to my partner sustaining a spiral fracture to his hand, an injury serious enough that he never got back in the car with me again. He did go on, though, to a successful run in the investigative sections of our department.

Meanwhile, I was left without my patrol partner, who was also a long-time friend. That put me in an emotionally vulnerable spot on Valentine's night when I was involved in the pursuit of a stolen car. In the middle of the chase, the stolen car collided with and killed a totally innocent married couple in the heart of downtown Saskatoon. All of the defence mechanisms I had been using up until that point were overwhelmed. My dam had burst. Without the support of my friend and long-time partner at the accident scene, I felt totally devastated, alone, and isolated.

It was no one's fault and that's just the way things happen sometimes. But I had seniority at this point. I was a leader and, because I felt it was important no one knew or suspected how I felt, I covered up my pain. I was affected deeply and changed by what had happened, though. I just couldn't admit it.

Except for my family, most people didn't know I was struggling. I threw myself back into policing and worked even harder to prove to myself I was all right. All of my fallbacks and coping methods were changing as well. The kids were growing up and in school, and my wife was working. They didn't have time or want to spend every day with me. Bouts of anxiety caused me to panic sometimes when I was running, taking some of the therapeutic aspect out of long runs.

The second half of my career started out rough. The tumultuous events of the years 2000 to 2005 started when two police officers took an intoxicated Indigenous man out of town in subzero weather and abandoned him. This started a firestorm of accusations and inquiries. As I have mentioned earlier, the Saskatoon Police were investigated by the RCMP.

Allegations of racism and police brutality were everyday realities for officers on the streets. The climate of those years enabled me to not deal with the aftermath of the chase and the deaths of two innocent people back in 1999. The on-to-the-next-call mentality was back. My reaction to the chase had scared me, though. I knew at some level I wasn't immune to everything I was dealing with.

For families of serving first responders and all of the people involved in occupations where traumas and critical incidents are a part of their lives, I know it's hard to watch your loved ones change over time. I know from my own experience—my wife, mother, and other people close to me saw the subtle and not so subtle changes. Sometimes without words I could see the concern in their eyes.

If you suspect someone you love is suffering from posttraumatic stress, be patient but be persistent in your efforts to get them to talk about it. Expect them to be defensive and to hide behind confidentiality to deflect your efforts. Once I began talking about the effects the job had on me, the better I felt. I didn't name names or give up investigative details; I just told what happened. In the last years of my career, there wasn't a lot my wife and I didn't talk about. Talking about critical incidents after they have occurred is not the magic bullet, but it helps you process what you are thinking. Unfortunately, talking spreads the impact around, and, hopefully, the people who are listening to you are not too badly affected.

Talking about post-traumatic stress is one of the most positive steps we have taken in helping the helpers stay healthy. We know where we have made mistakes in the past and it enables us to anticipate and lessen the effects of post-traumatic stress. Knowing people have an idea and understand at least partially what you have experienced makes you a stronger person.

In the last years of my career, the frequency of critical incidents and the lack of time to recover in between wore me down. I knew I was becoming less capable of dealing with death, injured people, and survivors, even if no one else did. Unashamedly, I could say I had enough. The lingering effects of a violent trauma-filled career are still around. Sometimes I will get emotional over the weirdest things. The stories you would expect to trigger feelings—innocent people getting injured or killed, police officers being murdered, fatal accidents—can bring back buried feelings. But then there are unexpected occurrences that will trigger a reaction, like seeing someone who resembles a person who died violently. Smells, gestures, or noises can all trigger memories you thought you'd scrubbed. I know these things will be with me for many years to come. They aren't as scary when you experience them repeatedly.

For the people serving, I can offer some advice based on my experiences. Talking about post-traumatic stress doesn't make you weak. If anything, it will help you and make you more resilient. It will help you make it through your chosen career. Be critical in your self-assessment of your ability to deal with stress. If you've had enough, don't risk your long-term health by taking the next call before you are able to. Dealing with how you have been impacted by a trauma is always a very personal thing, but it becomes everyone else's business when it affects your ability to do your job effectively.

The more-with-less reality of most emergency services is a fiscal fact of life. It also increases the frequency of trauma exposure. If you are a leader in an emergency services trade, if at all possible, make sure the exposure to traumas isn't limited to the same group of people over and over. You are not alone, and more people than you know support and appreciate what you do. Take care of yourself so you can take care of others. No matter how well prepared, indoctrinated, and trained you are, real-life experiences will test you like you have never been tested before. I think most people who have left emergency response careers will tell you the hardest part after you leave is the guilt.

Survivor's guilt may be irrational in most cases, but it's there. You hear your former comrades and co-workers going through or experiencing a traumatic event and, even knowing you had done enough in the past, you still wish you could be there for them. Most parents understand this when it comes to their children. They would sooner suffer than see their children suffer. Veterans from all the wars expressed this sentiment many times in documentaries and in print. You eventually find a place for it. You have to. You owe it to your family and all the people who supported you over the years.

CHAPTER 14
WALK A KILOMETRE OR THIRTY—
MY NEW LIFE ON THE STREET

Once I had retired from the Saskatoon Police Service, I had more time to do different kinds of things. One of the projects I took on back in 2016 gave me a new perspective on my old job. I became involved in efforts to raise money for the Sanctum Care Group. Sanctum Care opened Saskatchewan's first transitional care home and hospice for people with HIV/AIDS in November 2015. I helped with a fundraiser to establish a ten-bed, pre-natal care home to support high-risk, HIV-positive pregnant women. The ultimate goal was to prevent the transmission of HIV to the unborn child during and after pregnancy by providing a stable environment and high-quality care.

The fundraiser was the brainchild of the creators of Sanctum, a team of community-minded doctors, health care professionals, and members of the community who strongly believe all people with HIV, especially those who are homeless, have a better chance of longevity with a stabilized, caring environment. What Sanctum is doing is important because Saskatchewan has one of the highest rates of HIV infection in Canada, thanks in large part to intravenous drug use.

When I was first approached to take part, I was apprehensive. The fundraiser was loosely based on the popular television series *Survivor*. The premise was that ten local celebrities would live on the streets of Saskatoon for thirty-six hours with no ID or money. We'd be allowed cellphones but only to update social media about our experiences. We'd also be required to complete challenges designed to highlight what homeless people face every day. These challenges would involve obstacles surrounding obtaining medical care for people with HIV/AIDS.

The biggest obstacle for me was to overcome my own feelings and experiences about the consequences of IV drug use I'd experienced when I was a police officer. I really wrestled with this, since so much misery and pain is caused by illegal IV drug use, which is made possible by organized crime and street gangs. This disease was being spread by the kind of crime I used to fight on the streets of Saskatoon, a fact that left me feeling seriously conflicted.

What got me past this hurdle was my first visit to a Sanctum facility, where I met the residents. I'd dealt with many of them or knew their families from my previous career. There was no room for animosity after the visit and tour. The residents were no longer a threat to anyone and had embraced the goodwill extended to them. Sanctum offered them a peaceful place and quality of life they needed to get their lives in order so they could manage their conditions.

The second turning point was the idea and information provided to me, highlighting the fact that high-risk pregnant women with HIV could, in the right circumstances, have children without transmitting the virus to them. The child would stay with the mother after being born and not become a ward of the province. A woman who conquered her addictions while receiving pre-natal care, even while having HIV, could raise a child without the risk of passing on the virus. They could stay together and live as a family. That, to me, was the greatest benefit of this initiative.

The next major obstacle was the real and ever-present danger, as an ex-police officer, of being on the streets where a chance encounter with some criminals and gang members looking for an opportunity to settle old grievances would be too good to pass up. Some serving members of the Saskatoon Police and some of my own family members advised against taking such a risk. I didn't think of myself as a local celebrity, or even a prominent citizen, so I wondered if lending my name to the fundraiser would be of any worth. I also knew I'd be terrible at asking people for money.

The last, and certainly not the least, of my concerns was walking around in the area where I had so many memories. To me, it was like kicking at ghosts. I have memories from many places in Inner City Saskatoon. Many of those memories are of traumatic, tragic, and violent incidents. It seemed like a provocation to revisit them once again. But then I reached a tipping point when I thought of a child born to a mother with HIV who had been stabilized and was able to raise the child like any other mother. The child wouldn't enter the care of anyone else and be kept out of the system.

That was enough for me. I was in.

Still, in the weeks leading up to the challenge, I had bouts of anxiety and wondered if I did the right thing by committing to this. On the other hand, I couldn't help but be impressed—and a little intimidated—by the diversity of the other participants as they were confirmed. There was a doctor, a nurse, a politician, a reporter, two well-known musicians, the Roman Catholic bishop of Saskatoon, the chief of the Saskatoon Tribal Council, and the head of the Métis Urban Council. Again, I was sure I'd be a terrible fundraiser, especially compared to these guys.

There were more nerves in the last week before the event. I really began to wonder if the Sanctum Care Group could pull this off successfully. From my point of view, it was a hard sell for people not directly involved in Sanctum's work. But then it all seemed to come together. The local paper in Saskatoon ran an online article just prior to the fundraiser and, clearly, the community was engaged. Some of the online commentary on the story was positive and supportive. Some was mean-spirited, denigrating the fundraiser by saying the participants in the challenge were just playing at being homeless and exploiting their plight.

The critics were missing the point. All of us in this challenge knew we were only getting a taste of the trials homeless people face every day. I think we were all realistic about what we were doing. The point was to raise money and awareness for a specific purpose and not to replicate the conditions people faced with 100 percent accuracy. Still, some of the comments stung and, if we let them, they could have taken the wind out of our sails. There was even some personal attacks on me. But you just have to shake that stuff off and stick to the mission at hand.

On the day of the challenge, we reported to the Sanctum residence at six a.m. and met the other participants, some for the first time. My partner for the next thirty-six hours had, apparently, drawn the short straw. Danielle Chartier is an NDP member of the Saskatchewan Legislature who was just starting her third term at the time of the event. Danielle also represents the riding where we would be spending most of our time.

We were given a sheet with our challenges and tasks. Each team had different goals, so we wouldn't tie up resources for people or overcrowd offices. All of the challenges required walking, so we tried to keep them sequential. Our first challenge was making an appointment with a doctor without a health card or identification. We went to the Westside Medical Clinic and, after asking to see a doctor, we sat in a crowded, busy waiting room. The staff told us it was actually quiet for a Friday.

Some people recognized me and made comments about how my shoes looked too new for me to be homeless. That was funny because they were runners from Walmart and they were about five years old. One fellow told me he and his friends would find where I was sleeping at night. I thought to myself, "If you want to come after me at night, I'll see you then." Most people, however, were supportive. Becoming invisible would be difficult in some of the places we were required to try to access services, but I knew it would happen as we went along.

We had an opportunity to speak to a doctor after about forty-five to fifty minutes. He explained that seeing patients without health cards or identification was only the start. If the patient required further treatment or tests, these were unobtainable without a health card and difficult to coordinate without an address.

Creativity and innovative methods only go so far in obtaining health care. As we went through the challenges, the recurring theme was not having identification or a fixed address—both major obstacles to accessing any services. At the same time, there were many people who did their best to help. They too face challenges, managing finite resources, knowing what mental health issues face those in need, and handling it all while not getting overwhelmed or discouraged by the circumstances.

Danielle and I couldn't have been more opposite in our political views, so we left that out of our conversations for the most part as we walked from challenge to challenge. We walked approximately eighteen kilometres on the first day alone. That's something you wouldn't think would be too difficult for people like us who were healthy. Also, the weather was nice. But walking to every challenge ate up our day, and each task we completed only got us to the next. The daily ritual of trying to get food, medical care, and housing took up all of our time, so there wasn't much opportunity to make progress in any other areas to improve the quality of our lives.

We made a stop at AIDS Saskatoon to see if we could use its address as a mailing address when we were trying to obtain identification. The health bus and the food bank were on our list as well. We only took water from the food bank, but we learned we could have received a three-day emergency food basket without identification if we needed it.

The food bank was one of the busiest places we stopped at. All ages, genders, and races were there, picking up hampers to make ends meet. It was a powerful and telling moment for me. The numbers of people accessing the food bank were also staggering. I'd grown a little cynical in the latter part of my career about some of the people who access the food bank. Some food bank users, as learned during my policing days, are gang members and drug dealers, who were just taking advantage (as they are often inclined to do) of the people and organizations that contributed to the food bank. But I didn't see anyone like that when I was there.

Danielle and I were separated for the night. I then linked up with four other men participating in the challenge and we made our way to a local park. It was a long and sleepless night. The foot traffic in the park was constant and some people were intoxicated. Many of them wanted to talk and were curious about four middle-aged men sleeping, or trying to sleep, on the ground.

Unlike me, all of the other participants with me that evening had the internet on their phones and updated their social media before turning in for the night. Some of the updates were very insightful and some darkly humorous. Bishop Don Bolen tweeted he knew why some homeless people sleep on the streets in the daytime—downtown parks are just too busy at night.

The next day, one thing Danielle and I were in absolute agreement on was the leadership lessons we were learning during the challenge. Clearly, there was a need to streamline some services and effectively marshal resources for lower income and homeless people. The costs of duplication, noncommunication, and unnecessary bureaucracy in the long run outweigh what the costs would be if we made some changes now. No person in our community should be allowed to become virtually invisible and fall through the cracks when we have systems in place to help.

Some of the people who worked for these organizations echoed our sentiments. I've written about checking your ego in the police leadership world. It's equally as important for leaders in community outreach and support organizations to do the same. Effective leaders who don't mind who gets the credit can accomplish a lot and get the job done.

I know the Sanctum Survivor challenge offered only a glimpse at the realities of so many people in Saskatoon, including homeless people. It happened in June, not in the most bitterly cold months when the suffering of people on the street has to be at its worst. It was the first time an event like this had been attempted in Saskatoon, and I believe it raised awareness in the city. It gave us all some perspective.

During the challenge, I had the privilege of meeting community leaders who I may never have had a chance to meet in normal circumstances. We all brought different viewpoints and experiences with us, and we will carry those new perspectives back to the people we will encounter in the future. Overall, the experience was worthwhile.

I thought I knew a lot about the difficulties and challenges people face as a former police officer, but there was still much more to learn during the challenge. I also knew a lot of the people we encountered, but the experience filled in a lot of gaps in my thinking and helped to make a more complete picture for me of what goes on every day for people living on the street.

At the end of it all, Danielle posted a comment on social media that summed things up well. She wrote that every elected politician involved in social services, justice, health, policing, and corrections should have to take part in an experience like this if they want to be effective. She added the advice that, if you want to be a good leader and make changes, you need to experience at least some of what the people you serve do. I couldn't have said it better myself.

As a postscript, I am very happy to say the ground was broken and construction started on the new permanent Sanctum hospice in the spring of 2018. The third Sanctum Survivor challenge took place a month later.

CHAPTER 15
GETTING PAST "I DON'T LIKE COPS"– MY LIFE AS A WRITER

In July 2016, I was invited to my first multi-day writers' festival in Moose Jaw, Saskatchewan, called the Festival of Words. It was a totally new experience for my wife and me—a celebration of writing, ideas, and people who loved the written or spoken word. On the first evening, I was one of the writers chosen to do a reading as part of a panel to kick off the festivities.

That night an artist who was an award-winning spoken word poet took the stage. I had never seen or heard a spoken word artist before his performance. He was mesmerizing. He recited a powerful poem in a strong, steady, and rhythmic voice. I can say without hesitation it was one of the most powerful deliveries of an idea I heard in years. As he was winding down, perfectly within his allotted time, an entirely selfish thought came into my head: "Please don't let me be after him." He finished to a thunderous round of well-deserved applause and then…they called my name.

My wife Christine, who has been in many respects my most supportive coach, critic, and fan, had been telling me since I started this writing journey, "If you are invited as a writer, read from your books when presenting." So that night I did. And I think I did all right. The spoken word poet and I presented very different genres, but I think the festival organizers were right on the money by presenting us back to back.

The festival was well organized, and the twenty-eight writers and artists involved that year were paired up at various venues in the downtown of Moose Jaw. People could choose who they wanted to come and hear. I was thrilled to be paired up that day with successful and experienced professional writers. I learned so much about presenting. When I first started presenting, the only thought I had was this: "I can't believe people asked me to come and talk." Being with professional artists was an eye-opener. Totally confident, they read and spoke without any hesitation.

On the second day of the festival I was paired up with the spoken word poet for another session. I deferred to him and let him go ahead of me because, as a performer, he had the seniority. When we were finished our presentations, there was an allotted time for questions from the audience. The first question was to the point. A lady asked, "Why do you think the festival organizers put you two together?"

Once again, I deferred to the spoken word artist and passed him the microphone. He took it and answered, "I don't like cops," and then handed the microphone back to me. The room went silent.

I was more than two years out of policing and just starting to accept I was a writer. Though my subject matter was mostly about policing, I had written and spoken about leadership, empathy, and many other things. I don't know if he said what he said with genuine malice in his heart, or if he was just looking for a reaction. Either way, in the setting of a book festival, it was provocative.

Under pressure many times before, I have learned the first response is often the most honest. I cannot remember my exact words. But I basically replied that I love this country we live in, where we are free to express ourselves even if our opinions are contrary to those held by others. Afterwards, when speaking with the spoken word artist and members of the audience, I was struck by how much my former career can polarize some people. People can freely express how they feel about police officers without ever seeing the person beneath the uniform.

Once you have been a soldier or a police officer, no matter where life takes you afterwards, in your heart you will always relate your experiences to those years. I suppose it's the same with any former vocation if you were passionate about what you did. I am now five years into my retirement from policing and five years into my career as a writer. Both careers are intertwined because I have written about my experiences as a police officer as my introduction to writing.

I am not a blame or I-told-you-so guy. I might have been a bit when I was younger, but now I just let things play out and hope a lesson is learned in the end run. Police officers who retired before I did used to say when you retire it's "twenty feet or twenty seconds, that's how long the job will remember you when you walk out the door."

I used to think this was a harsh analogy. In retrospect, though, there was a lot of truth to it. When you leave a job like policing, the intensity of the job continues without you. New challenges, new crimes, new criminals, new police officers, new and constant changes in laws: you are no longer a part of the inner circle. Confidential information and investigations cannot be the fodder to coffee talk when and if you do meet up with officers who are still serving after you retire.

Writing about policing from my own perspectives and experiences so a person who has never been a police officer has a better idea how police think and why they do what they do has been rewarding. Movies and television don't portray the actual day-to-day workings of a police service—probably because it wouldn't be very entertaining. The big cases, the sensational crimes, and any mistakes the police make are always highlighted somewhere. The day-to-day operations and how well they are conducted is where the strength of any police service can be effectively measured.

"I don't like cops" was a powerful statement. But it turned out it was also a validation for me as a writer. As part of its theme in 2016, the Festival of Words had highlighted three words: "inspiration," "investigation," and "instruction." Mission accomplished.

The summer after that festival, I received a letter from the Saskatoon Police Service, indicating all municipal police forces in Saskatchewan would soon be subject to a new act requiring them to add a new level of protection to the privacy of people the police deal with. As a result, the police service was requesting that I turn over all my police notebooks and any copies of police reports I had in my possession. I had kept all of my notebooks from the date I had started until I retired from the Saskatoon Police in October 2013. I used them to fact-check stories I had written about in my books. I missed the first deadline to comply with the request.

I struggled with the idea of turning over the notebooks because they were my connection with all I had experienced over the years. Some were terrible reminders of tragedy, and some were my personal documentation of events I was proud of. At the Stonechild Inquiry into the death of a seventeen-year-old First Nations youth under questionable circumstances, I was one of the few officers who actually had notes. Now a police officer's notes must be permanently retained, but back then, prior to the inquiry, police officers with the Saskatchewan police services were only required to retain their notebooks for seven years before they could be destroyed. I kept my notebooks and it stood me in good stead.

I also kept the only existing copy of the report compiled by the Saskatoon Police investigators during their investigation—such as it was—into the sudden death of the young man. The report became the basis of the inquiry and prevented sweeping allegations and theories from taking over.

So hanging onto my notebooks had, in the past, a deeper and more powerful outcome than I could have imagined. Now this letter, delivered almost four years after I had left the police, was asking me to surrender—just in case they are needed—all of my police notebooks.

I tried to articulate the reasons why I should retain them and wondered if I could make a reasoned argument to keep them in my possession. I wondered if there was a legal way of challenging this request. When I thought about it more, though, I could see how it could create a bad precedent, because any police officer who had something to hide could refuse to turn over their notebooks. I had nothing to hide. I just wanted them for personal reasons.

In October 2017, I received a second follow-up letter. I had spent most of my adult life enforcing the law and I wasn't going to begin breaking it because of my stubbornness or pride. Five days before the deadline, I went downstairs and pulled the boxes out. I checked them year-by-year to make sure they were all there.

A tombstone preceded the first notes of each shift. The date and time of my shift start, and my partner's name and badge number if I had one. My assignment and duty hours were recorded. My patrol sergeant's and the watch commander's names and my car and portable radio number were all neatly written down. The weather was noted all before writing down wanted or missing persons. Any other information the watch commander provided usually went in the book before the shift started. They were a template of friends and co-workers. Some of the officers and senior officers have passed on, but all of these people were my other family for years. We had a common bond of experiences few people will ever have. People you liked and people you didn't. People you had forgotten were suddenly there to see as I flipped through the books. Every day and every night the ritual was the same. Record the tombstone information to start your shift. Every day I worked—it was all there.

Looking through all these notebooks was a melancholy task. I saw my blood dried on a few pages where I had written my notes with shaky bloodied hands after a violent arrest. I picked up more than a few cuts from contacting gravel or broken glass in a scrum. There were pages where the ink had run because of sweat after a foot chase. There were notes that were faint because it was so cold the pens we were issued could barely write.

There were spontaneous utterances and confessions written in quotations before the days of video, which were almost always challenged in court. Countless names, dates of birth, addresses, and phone numbers were recorded. Crucial times were written at the start of every call: the time of the call or the time the incident was dispatched or the time an on view occurred (an *on view* is when you have actually witnessed a crime in progress or contacted a suspicious person without being dispatched to the call). My notes also recorded the time of arrival, the time of an arrest, or any other significant event that occurred while I was there. Sometimes the notes were neat and other times it was a hasty scrawl across the page.

On the side of the pages an incident number was recorded and any cross-referenced occurrences were written. At the end of each of the thousands of calls, a solid line across the bottom of the page separated each incident from the next. The names were what really stood out. So many people alive and dead. People whose faces and stories I can still remember. Many names were repeats, but I was always good with that. I knew them, and they knew me at some level.

I could see my personal progression as an officer as I went from year to year. My first notebooks were rich in detail, most of which was not required. My notes were always neatly written. In a couple of years, I was down to "just the facts," but that didn't mean my notes were shorter. It was just the opposite: I knew what to look for and what to record. "Just the facts," once you are more seasoned, grew to many pages.

The books smelled musty from the basement and many were yellowed. The elastics used to bind them had dried and sometimes fell off in flakes of dessicated rubber (a logical consequence of the city using the lowest bidder to supply its elastics). I arranged them by year in separate piles and, once they were all accounted for, placed them in boxes.

I knew I would have to turn in my notebooks and entrust them to people I did and didn't know. Trust was an earned commodity with me over the years. I didn't know what safeguards were put in place after the Stonechild Inquiry, and I would have to trust they would be sufficient. Once I was done and all of the notebooks were boxed, I put them out of my thoughts until the next day. The next morning after the gym, I loaded them into the truck and drove them to the station. It was a Sunday, so no one except the patrol shift was on duty. It turned out to be my old platoon and I was met by a sixteen-year veteran. He was busy, so a young constable with three years' experience took my books. I felt bad for the kid as he would have to do an occurrence report and enter them into exhibits. After he gave me a photocopy of the letter I received, I was done.

Two hundred and fifty-six notebooks and twenty-six years of policing memories in my own handwriting were gone. I thought I would be more upset, but I wasn't. On November 5, 2017, I think I decided, in spite of all my hesitation and self-doubt, that despite the fact I had given up years of memories in those notebooks, I was going to be an all-in writer.

The nice thing about being a writer and a reader is having the ability to write or read the whole story. Writing and reading gives you a clearer picture of emotional or conversational events and allows for a fuller perspective. Reading has never been more important or relevant as it is now. Electronic and social media lets people pick and choose with lightning speed what parts of stories fit their viewpoint or what they are most comfortable with. When writing, I have sometimes surprised myself with where my views on some subjects truly are. When reading, I am often enlightened and walk away with "I never thought of it that way before." I am absolutely honoured that people have been reading my first two books and feel humbled by it. Experience is a commodity all leaders should share without expectations. Everyone has a story worth telling or hearing, if for no other reason than to give a different perspective to someone else.

Since the books came out, I have been approached by many people and asked for advice on writing and getting published. I always feel guilty when I relate my experience to them. I decided to write the first book, *Indian Ernie: Perspectives on Policing and Leadership*, after being encouraged by my peers in the police service. It seemed a logical way to pass on the things I had learned throughout my life and career.

It began humbly enough by handwriting stories into old, unused, school notebooks (my girls skipped a lot of school, so there were a lot of them lying around the basement). After

I had written about one hundred pages of stories, I began to show them to my kids and friends, who encouraged me to keep going. Ever wary, I wondered if they were encouraging me so as not to hurt my feelings, thinking I would eventually get discouraged and abandon the project.

I think every writer feels that uncertainty when they begin writing. I decided the one sure way to keep me committed was to tell everyone I was writing a book. Once you have announced you are writing a book, you had better do it. You don't want to be the person who gets asked "how is your book coming along?" years after you announced you were writing one. That is, unless you're an academic who has to do years of research before you can put the last period on paper to finish your book.

I was still working as a police officer, so finding time to write was a challenge. I wrote most of the book in the mornings after night shift, before everyone was awake, or I'd write in the afternoon when my family was at work or school. There were so many distractions and, life being what it is, I began to get discouraged. The big test of the viability of the book was to show some of the stories to the harshest critics: other police officers. I started with the special constables who worked in the detention area of the Saskatoon Police Service. They were a captive audience, so to speak. My next victim was a supervisor in central records who typed many of the thousands of reports I had left over the years. She was also an avid reader. I'm indebted to them always for their encouragement and approval. Once I truly believed I had stories people could read and be engaged by, the rest of the book came pretty quickly.

When I thought I was done, I went on the internet and looked up how to get a book published. Many publishers have extensive guidelines and formats for submissions, which were daunting to a novice. Some only wanted an outline of the book or a sample chapter and gave no guarantees on a timeline as to when they might possibly look at your work. Many stated quite clearly that the number of submissions they received exceeded their capacity to review them in a timely matter, and that it could be up to a year before you would even receive a rejection.

Other publishers wouldn't look at your work if you had sent it to any of their competitors, so a writer couldn't use the shotgun approach. Some had cost-share programs, where the aspiring writer had to assume some of the financial risk of getting a book in print. Encouraged by all the impersonal and restrictive conditions, I made up my mind to look at local Saskatchewan publishers. If I was going to be rejected, I wanted to be right away so I could get back to policing without having pipe dreams about being a writer. I wanted to meet the person who judged my efforts, because I'm a little old-fashioned that way.

My wife Christine was amazingly patient with me as I was writing and then looking for a publisher. Revisiting traumatic events while I was writing made for some interesting nights and both of us losing sleep. Anyone who is married to an aspiring or published writer will tell you it comes with its own set of unique challenges. My analogy for the early part of this journey is crossing over a frozen lake in late spring. Every step is fraught with peril and uncertainty as you negotiate the ice, and even if you get across safely you still don't know what waits on the other side.

I found Purich Publishing shortly after I began searching for Saskatchewan publishers. I went on its website and looked at its titles. I wasn't encouraged because most of the books were academic publications. Purich was in Saskatoon, however, and its website stated it published books on Aboriginal issues, law, social justice issues, and western history. After searching the books listed in each category, I found an out-of-print book about a Native rodeo rider. I decided I had a chance.

I called the number on the website and nervously told Karen Bolstad who I was and that I had written a book. She listened patiently and told me to send the whole thing via email. I compared it later to a cheesy guy in a Camaro with a mullet driving up to a stranger on the street, winking, and expecting them to come for a ride.

The next step for aspiring writers is the wait until the publisher has reviewed your work. Fortunately, I was still working full-time so I had a lot to keep me distracted. But waiting was still difficult, and I began to second-guess myself whenever things were quiet. Eventually, I was contacted and a meeting was set up at the home of Don Purich and Karen, as they were a home-based publisher. For any new writers, be prepared for the question, "Who did you write this book for?"

I had never really thought about who my intended audience was going to be. I would have been happy if anyone read it. I fumbled my way through the meeting and came away with the feeling the first book was going to happen. Don, Karen, and a young lady working on her PhD, who was interning for the summer, each wrote a memorandum on the manuscript, detailing its weaknesses and strengths. It was pretty clear there was going to be more work and commitment required to bring the book to print.

So back to the manuscript I went, trying to address its weaknesses first. This was completely foreign to me. I wasn't a good student, so it goes without saying I wasn't good at homework either. Whenever the opportunity allowed, I tried to fix or revise the raised issues. There was a flurry of back and forth emails and it was getting done. I realized I was asking a lot of a small publishing company to commit to publishing an unknown writer. It was taking a chance on me and on a book different from most books in its catalogue. Unlike the big publishing companies, every project or undertaking is a significant drain on time and limited resources for small publishers.

When I had done enough work, I got a call to have a meeting to sign a contract. I was ecstatic. We arranged to meet after one of my night shifts in late June 2013. On the Friday night shift before the meeting, I was involved in a violent arrest and cracked two ribs, among other injuries. So on the Monday I gingerly went to lunch with Don and Karen and told them the story about the arrest and signed a contract. I was given until December to reduce the size of the manuscript to a trade book format (approximately two hundred pages). At the meeting, I said I was going to retire from policing. It was the first time I had ever said the words out loud to anyone. I had been saying for years to officers considering retirement that once you say the words out loud, you were committed and there was no going back.

I literally floated home after signing the contract, forgetting all about my cracked ribs. In a matter of days, I had the manuscript down to an acceptable size. I was off the street for the next few weeks, recuperating from my injuries, and found myself working in the watch commander's office. The next few weeks were a blur. I didn't submit the paperwork to retire for a couple of months, but I knew I was done.

The editing of the manuscript was next. After I received the first edit, with red and blue bubble notes alongside the written text, I felt like I was looking at my first Grade 9 math exam. Young writers, don't get discouraged if your work at this stage comes back with a lot of new ink. It's a learning process. Depending on what you are writing about, you may have to explain certain terms and processes if the general public is not familiar with them. You will miss connecting words and break writing structure rules you didn't even know existed unless you were an English major. You will be asked what ideas you are trying to convey and to justify some of your opinions or views. Editors can crush a writer's soul if you take it personally. However, it's not personal. It's part of the process of having a book published.

Once you sign off on the edited version, you have to step back because no more changes are going to happen. The next steps are the design and selecting a cover. Choosing what pictures if any are going to be included is a fun process. In my second book, I wrote about how the majority of pictures in both my first and second books came from the *Saskatoon StarPhoenix*.

Finally, the book goes to the printers for its first, and hopefully not last, printing run. I can tell you that seeing your first book in print after coming from the printers is pretty intoxicating. Freshly printed books in a box have a smell similar to the new car smell everyone remembers was how Karen Bolstad described it.

There are other bumps and turns in the process: legal and defamatory concerns, whether or not your book is nonfiction; copyright issues; and funding issues, but Purich Publishing covered those unthought-of issues for me. The benefits of having your publisher in the same area code cannot be overstated.

Launching your work brings back all the anxieties you had when you first started it. Hopefully, you will have success and not get slammed by the literary critics. People will read and like your book. I want to revisit what I said at the beginning of this chapter. The beauty of being a writer is the ability to explain in detail what you have experienced. After the first book came out, people who asked me how I wrote it and got it published often asked the questions in situations where time didn't allow me to explain everything. Writing gives me a better opportunity than I could have hoped for.

First off, I got lucky. I met the right people at the right time. If you're a writer, you can create your own luck by being passionate about what you are writing. Finding the right people means doing the work. Research publishers and what they are looking for. Expect disappointments and rejections—just because you like what you have written doesn't mean everyone else will.

I recently read a book by Max Braithwaite called *The Night We Stole the Mountie's Car*. It gathers the recollections of Max, a Depression-era teacher who wants to be a writer. Every chapter has a story about the rejection slips he receives, and they all come in the mail. But he keeps at it. Max Braithwaite wrote a story he was passionate about and based it on his real-life experiences. He became a best-selling and award-winning author through persistence.

Find your passion, write with abandon, and do the research on potential publishers when you're done. What happens after the book comes out will be different for everyone.

Being a published writer can be interesting and rewarding, but there is a business aspect to it as well. Not knowing a lot about the publishing industry and its day-to-day operations, I've learned a lot in the past couple of years. I was fortunate Purich Publishing was only a few kilometres' drive from my home. I know now how unique of a situation I was in as a writer. Then came a surprise I never expected or anticipated.

In late November 2015, Karen and Don invited my wife and me to lunch. We met them in a restaurant close to our respective homes. We were presented with a letter. The letter detailed how Purich Publishing had been sold to an out-of-province academic publisher, University of British Columbia Press, or UBC Press. Don and Karen wanted to go into semi-retirement. The sale was effective at the beginning of December that year. I was happy for them and proud of all they had achieved as an independent, home-based, publishing company in a publishing world dominated by giants. But Saskatchewan writers were losing a very valuable and unique company.

My analogy after the initial shock was I had been traded. I was playing for the Saskatchewan Roughriders on Friday and, starting Monday, I was with the BC Lions. But like a hard-working pro football player, I survived and thrived. And I kept looking for outlets for my writing, which led me, dear reader, to University of Regina Press and the book you're reading now. (It turns out I'm back with the Riders.)

CHAPTER 16
THE FIRST TIME MY FATHER AND I HUNTED TOGETHER

I love my father. But we've had an unconventional relationship. My parents divorced when I was young. The divorce was not amicable, as far as I could tell. My mother rarely talked about my father. I went to my father's home a few times as a young boy. He'd remarried and had moved on by then. The first memories I have of him are from Kaquatosh, a small community in northern Ontario. I don't know why he was there or what job he was doing there. I do remember the roads were made of sand, and we lighted the house we lived in by Coleman lanterns, as opposed to the coal oil lamps we used at my mother's house.

The next memories of my father are from Sault Ste. Marie on the Garden River First Nation, where I went after a daylong train trip on the Algoma Central Railway. I knew so little of my father that his new wife acted as an intermediary between us. My sister was born to my father and stepmother around this time, and I quickly faded into the background.

My father was a hard worker. He worked for a construction company and had risen to foreman. He was very proud of the fact he was a foreman. I was too young to see or appreciate the dynamics of a son from a first marriage living with a new family and soon I went back to live with my mother. I did feel, though, that I didn't belong in their new life and I accepted he had moved on.

My sister reached out several times when she was a little girl, but being a young man I was more concerned with other things in my life. The moment I remember most vividly was when she wrote me letters when I was overseas in Cyprus, peacekeeping with the Canadian Forces. In the scrawl of a child, she tried to make me understand I was her big brother—she needed to know if I knew this. She was a little girl looking for a big brother and, though I wrote her back, I missed the chance to be what she needed.

Life being what it is, my father and his family and I grew further apart. My father was quiet during this period and I came to resent his silence. My sister became a nurse and had a baby girl.

All the things and talk that come with divorce manifested themselves over the years. I had become so self-reliant by this point I didn't give any of this a lot of thought. My wife is also a child of divorce, and she told me I shouldn't be so rigid in my positions. She encouraged me to be more open-minded about my father and his new life. By then I was settled in Saskatoon and starting my own family. But, like so many people and families who live far apart and are living separate lives, it took a tragedy to bring us closer.

The Saskatoon Police Service had been entering a team for several years in a competition called the Louis Riel Race. It was one of the premier summer events in Saskatoon for years. A field of twenty or more teams took part. The race was an elaborate relay, encompassing canoeists, runners, horsemen, hill climbers, and then a final canoe race over a five-kilometre distance. Tens of thousands of people lined the riverbanks to watch and cheer on the teams. There was music and food for the spectators and an intense party atmosphere.

Of course, there was an unspoken rivalry between two of the most competitive teams, the firefighters and police. We police, though, knew we didn't stand a chance because the firefighters had way more time to train. After every competition, we would go to one of the relay member's homes for a barbeque and refreshments. It was a great team building and bonding event in which our families all took part. In 1997 it was our turn to host the after-party.

The race that year was eventful because the police team capsized our canoe in the initial river sprint while jostling with other canoes. So our bow paddler swam the baton into shore to the pack runner. Even with the setback, I thought we had a respectable finish. Tanned and tired, everyone headed to my home to celebrate. When I walked in the door, my wife looked upset. Our friend was with her, preparing for the barbeque and getting ready to greet people. I didn't know what was going on. My wife took me upstairs and told me my sister had been killed in a traffic accident on the highway between Timmins and Sault Ste. Marie in northern Ontario. My niece was with her, but she'd survived.

Because of the distance between Saskatoon and Sault Ste. Marie, I knew it would be a day or two until I could get there. I asked my wife and our friend not to tell the rest of the team yet until I knew more. Years later, my wife told me everyone already knew what had happened. Almost all people who have lost someone unexpectedly can tell you the numbness and shock erases details.

The next week was a blur of emotion and tears. It was the first time in all my years I had seen my father emotionally expressive.

He and his wife were in such pain I feared for their well-being. My niece was still in shock and spoke very little. My sister was my father's only child from his second marriage and my niece was young, so I broached the idea that she should come and live with us. We already had a full house and she would fit right in.

My sister's mother was adamant, though, that they would raise my niece. I understood and came back to Saskatoon. Our relationship changed after that painful summer and for the better too. We talked frequently on the phone, keeping each other posted on what was going on in our lives. Then my father shocked me by making the long drive to Saskatoon to stay with us several times over the next few years. He and his wife even came on the train on one occasion, and my partner and I picked them up from the train station in a patrol car one busy New Year's Eve.

One time my son answered the phone and it was my father asking for directions as they had driven up unannounced and he was in the city and didn't know how to get to our place from where he was. I began to know this other side of my family as I never had before. My father's sense of humour and world views surprised me.

I knew the real test for the male bonding in our family was the moose hunt. I stopped hunting after I joined the army and policing gave me all the thrills I needed. I'm averse to killing anything, unless it's really required, and food was abundant in my life, so I didn't need to hunt. It was, however, very important to my father that we should hunt together. It was an affirmation of who we were as men. Northerners will understand this. I had to become a moose hunter to seal the deal.

I took the train to northern Ontario and knew it was time to ante up. Before I left, I had been on a roll at work with arrests, including arresting a suspect wanted for an attempted murder, so I was feeling confident. Once in Ontario, we started the hunt in a beat-up old truck that leaked exhaust into the cab. My father was almost giddy, and I worried it was the carbon monoxide seeping into the cab.

We had only gone a few kilometres when we came to a small bridge at a blind corner. I slowed down and moved to the right because lumber trucks used the same roads. As I turned the curve, I saw a bull and cow moose standing on the road fifteen or twenty metres in front of us. The bush at the curve had prevented them from seeing us until the very last second. I stopped the truck and my father jumped out and started shooting at the bull, all the while yelling at me to shoot the cow.

I had to pull off the road, exit the vehicle, and load my rifle. My dad was running, shooting, and reloading on the run, something I'd never seen him do before. Twenty-five years my senior and he was running, shooting, reloading, and yelling like a teenager. I was trying not to laugh as I climbed up a slope to get my bearings.

The moose had run into an area where the trees had been harvested a couple of years earlier. I saw my father going after the bull, and I saw he had hit it at least twice. I saw the cow going in the opposite direction, about a hundred metres away. I sighted on her shoulder and fired. She fell instantly, and I saw the bull go down right afterwards. I walked through the uneven ground to where the cow fell. I fired once more to ensure she was dead and then went to check on my father and his bull. The bull was down, and my father was breathing heavily and very animated.

I went back to the cow and felt the sadness I always felt when I killed anything. I was glad for all the training and shooting I had done with the army and police services, which had enabled me to kill her quickly. I thanked her and went back to check on my father. His adrenaline was ebbing and he looked tired. We started laughing and then it began to sink in—we had a lot of work in front of us.

These two big beautiful animals had to be dressed and hauled out to the road. One moose is a lot of food and work; two is extraordinary. I knew no part of them would be wasted. Almost everyone who has ever tasted moose meat prefers it over all other meats. The sharing of moose meat is also a given social norm in northern Ontario.

As we worked through the day to get the moose hung up, alongside my stepfather who came out to give us a hand (he lived in the region and was another very accomplished hunter), I realized how important this hunt had been to my father. It meant acceptance and accomplishment for the two of us. If we had not done this together, it would have sat unresolved between us. It was the passing of the torch in many respects. My father could choose to stop hunting now, if he wanted to, because he had passed on the knowledge he had accumulated over the years to me.

There were so many lessons during this journey that started and ended with the sacrifice of the cow moose. When couples divorce, they aren't divorcing their children and those relationships should never be ignored because, if they are, there is a price. The price is lost opportunities to know people before they are lost to you, like my sister. Happily, her survivor, my niece, is married now and working as an optometrist. Like her mother the nurse, she wants to help people.

My father, meanwhile, while not without flaws, wanted and needed to hunt with me, because in the North so much of who you are as a man is defined by your ability to provide. I got the opportunity to know him and make up my own mind about who he was and what he was all about.

The strange world of having two families is all too common now for so many young people. It took me almost thirty years to have an open mind about this…and it had to be prompted by tragedy, but at least it was done. If there is someone out there you have a feeling you should connect with to make up your own mind, just do it and have no regrets.

POSTSCRIPT
ENOUGH SAID?

Significant events involving the Canadian justice system, which I used to work in, have occurred since I finished the first draft of this book. I'm often asked my opinion or to comment on them when I'm doing speaking engagements. I generally decline. Expressing my opinions in writing, though, allows me to state them to you calmly and precisely, so, bearing in mind what I said earlier in this book about us being blessed to live in a free country, here we go.

The opioid crisis has been an unfolding tragedy for years in Canada and abroad. I grieve for all the families affected. Not only the addicts but the families, the first responders, and the communities hardest hit. Some people blame the police for allowing this to happen. But organized crime groups are, for the most part, responsible for this tragedy and can only continue to reap profits as we divide our efforts. The police, who were among the first to raise this issue, continue to work on the opioid crisis quietly and without much fanfare. Hopefully, better days and solutions to this crisis will yet come.

The National Inquiry into Missing and Murdered Indigenous Women and Girls has also been unfolding much as I thought it would. There has been a movement by some to assign responsibility to and to blame the police. When I first heard the anti-police statements at the inquiry, I'll admit I was angry, but, ultimately, I know people just want to be heard. I am sure there have been instances where the police failed to investigate cases diligently and this warrants criticism. I also know from experience there will be many more cases where the police are not at fault. Unfortunately, unfairly assigning responsibility and blame and taking sides has become increasingly common in our connected and social media-driven society, but we must keep our sense of perspective.

And speaking of the power of online media, a recent headline I read suggested that every Indigenous young person should be afraid for their personal safety after Gerald Stanley in Saskatchewan and Raymond Cormier in Manitoba were both acquitted of killing First Nations young people. What kind of message is this for our youth? I have no doubt there are injustices that occur in our systems, but we can't give in to fear by suggesting every Indigenous young person should be fearful for their lives. Such suggestions I've seen online seem to me both irresponsible and wrong.

The fear around the Stanley and Cormier cases, of course, is tied up with the biggest hot button issue in Canada: racism. The last time I spoke to a recruit class at the Saskatchewan Police College, I addressed this by asking them point-blank: "How many of you are racists?" The look of shock on their faces was priceless! I then told them if they weren't racist, don't worry about being accused of being one. I explained if you're not, being called a racist—as a lot of them can expect to be called on the job—really doesn't mean anything.

Still, as an Indigenous man living in today's society, occasionally I do run into racism, which leads me to another story involving moose hunting. I was back in northern Ontario in 2017, hunting for moose in the area I grew up. I'm a treaty Indian and my band had won a decades-old court battle to hunt on the land they had been removed from to create a game preserve. So I was hunting where my ancestors had hunted.

Our lands make up one of the largest game preserves in Canada, but the north end of this territory is very isolated—only about seven or eight other people hunt there. Most hunters would think this would be an idyllic untouched paradise. The truth is, though, the area had been opened up to lumber companies for years before I ever had the right to hunt there. So when I go to hunt, I'm sharing the land with loggers. I still go, however, because it's a way of tying me to my past.

The lumber companies had carved many roads into the game preserve, which they regularly gated to prevent access to the areas where they were harvesting. Often over the years, since I have hunted, I've met trucks hauling loads of pulpwood as I've made my way to ridges and swamps where I would be hunting. I would pull well to the side of the narrow roads and let them pass. No one ever stopped to talk because they were paid by the load.

Every cutting crew usually had a foreman who travelled in a pickup truck, checking on the workers or marking off new areas to harvest. The first couple of years I was out there the foreman assigned to the area would stop to talk to me. After asking who I was and what I was doing there, he would carry on. However, he was a rude and abrupt man, and after he learned who my stepfather was, he went out of his way to tell me where beavers had dammed culverts and were creating a nuisance. My stepfather had the lumber company contract to trap nuisance beavers whose dams had flooded the roads.

Other than those conversations, I never really talked to him. The feeling I got from him was the roads were created for the purposes of hauling pulp and anyone on them who wasn't with his company was an irritant to him. I checked on this guy with a couple of other people. They all agreed he was just a company man who, by consensus, was not a friendly person. I had also heard more than a few times that other people in the area resented the fact that "Indians" could hunt on the game preserve. But the foreman never said anything to make me think he was part of that group.

On the weekends, when the pulp trucks weren't hauling, I could be out in the bush the entire day and never see another person. I've shot four moose over the five years I've been hunting there. But the 2017 hunt was beginning to feel like it was going to be another moose-free year for me, especially since I heard that other hunters who had come to the game preserve earlier in the season had all gone home empty-handed.

The weather was unusually warm, and I was hunting in a t-shirt with an orange safety vest and hat. I was pulled over by a small single-lane bridge, waiting for a haul truck to pass, when a new foreman for the area pulled up. I had never met him before. He was younger than the other guy, who had apparently retired. He had the same kind of look on his face, the look that asked, "What are you doing on our roads?"

Sure enough, he asked just that. I thought the orange hat and vest would have made it obvious. But I told him anyway; I was hunting. He then asked if I had gone past the gate they had erected a couple of kilometres up the road. I told him I had seen it the previous day, and that I also saw a truck parked about a kilometre past the gate at an awkward angle. So I went to see if everything was all right. It turned out it was one of the machine operator's trucks and everything was fine, so I drove straight out again.

Then, out of the blue and without missing a beat, the young man in the truck told me some "Natives" had broken through a gate at the south end of the game preserve. He said the lands and forests guys had dealt with them and no one got charged. He said it as factually and casually as if he was talking about the Toronto Maple Leafs losing a hockey game. I was used to casual racism in large settings, where people could just make their remarks and get away with moving on. In the setting we were in, though, his comment was brazen and totally out of order.

It occurred to me how deeply casual racism could be entrenched in someone over the course of their lives. I'm not a pacifist by any means, and I lived my professional life in an occupation where confrontation was an everyday requirement. But I chose not to confront him that day, and I simply asked him if he had seen any moose on his drive onto the game preserve. He told me he had not. I asked him some questions about how many trucks were hauling and how many men he had working for him.

The next day when he stopped, I asked where he was from and about his family. The day after that I asked him about how the contracts for pulp were secured and what the forecast for forestry operations was now that there was a trade dispute over softwood lumber. By the end of the week, we were drinking tea and spending twenty minutes talking before we parted ways.

There are times for confrontation and challenging people's beliefs, especially when the acts are overt and can cause harm. There are also times when a subtle approach can go much further and be more effective. I didn't get a moose on my 2017 fall hunt and the foreman had to go to Toronto before my last day of hunting, so I didn't see him before I left to come back to my home in Saskatchewan. I don't know if I changed his attitude or outlook, but I knew by the end of the week he saw me as a person worth talking to.

If there is an effective way to fight casual, off-the-cuff racist comments, I believe that letting the people who make them see you as a person has the most impact. In the isolated setting we were in, if the new young foreman hadn't come to see me as a person, he could have just driven by. He didn't. He stopped, each time talking with me longer than the last.

And we did it without social media, outrage, or bringing in other people to shore up our positions. Just two people who took race and racism out of the conversation on their own because one of us didn't allow it to be there. Remember: lead whenever and however you can.

APPENDIX 1
LEADERSHIP EVERYWHERE

A group of high school kids along with their teachers reminded me leadership comes in many forms. At the end of September 2016, I was having doubts about my writing and had stalled when I was close to finishing this book. I was checking my Twitter account and I saw a picture of the first book and a message from some students that were really enjoying it. They indicated they were starting a Twitter campaign to get me to come to their school. The students were from Wesmor Community High School in Prince Albert, Saskatchewan. I wasn't familiar with the school, and looking it up, I found it was a small high school with an enrollment of about three hundred students.

Because of its size, Wesmor is often overshadowed by the two other much larger high schools in Prince Albert. The school is at the end of a street in the West Flats area of the city. The West Flats area has a reputation as a tough neighbourhood with a high crime rate. Wesmor's student body is 95 percent Indigenous. I contacted one of the teachers and ended up going to the school in November 2016. I spoke to Grade 10, 11, and 12 kids and was absolutely inspired by them. They were attentive and asked great questions. Their leadership and initiative were what got me there. Without their efforts, I probably would have never heard of Wesmor Community High School and would have missed meeting some great young people and their dedicated teachers.

Sometimes leadership and leaders will just find you, and other times you have to look for them. If you are looking for leadership, in whatever you do, look in the mirror. Leadership and being successful starts with you. I have met many people who have said they don't like to be in charge or they don't want the responsibility. They have made a choice and in a backhanded kind of way are being leaders. To be a follower and allow someone to lead will make you a good judge of leadership. Eventually, being a good judge of leadership will lead you to positions of leadership.

One of the most powerful leadership traits is enthusiasm. I'm nothing if not enthusiastic. If you mix enthusiasm with optimism, you become a force to be reckoned with. I am optimistic about many things. I believe changes that have taken place just in my lifetime have, for the most part, been pretty positive. Changes in race relations, policing, and education have been happening steadily and sometimes go unnoticed. When we are caught up in the day-to-day activities of our lives, we somehow miss the changes.

Changes in language, interactions, and views can go unnoticed, except by the people around us. I see the changes in our youth. The messages and lessons our youth are receiving from the education system, from better-educated parents, and from so many other sources are powerful. While you may still have some holdouts, depending on what they are taught at home, most of the young people in Canada are more tolerant and inclusive.

The language of leadership is important. We have all worked with someone who was in a leadership position who never had anything good to say. Everything was negative, from the job to the equipment to the people. Negative language is very corrosive to young people. One negative comment can erase ten positive comments in a heartbeat.

As an Indigenous man, I think we need to change our leadership language. Words like "crisis," "hopelessness," and "desperate" should never be spoken by leaders when they can be heard or read by our youth. Grim and sometimes seemingly insurmountable problems will present themselves to you as a leader. Your language will be one of the first tools you can use to get past them.

When there is a problem affecting a whole community, its leaders reciting the problem in detail does nothing to reassure people—it's not leadership. Demanding or asking for help from people who have at best a tenuous connection to your community makes young people think we will get an easy or quick fix from external authorities. As generations of Indigenous leaders can tell you, this is simply not true.

I am a realist. I acknowledge there are some serious challenges to leaders in our communities and I do not pretend them away. Positive leadership language does more to empower young people and inspires them to work toward solutions.

Police, whether you like them or not, know there is no quitting when dealing with difficult or tragic circumstances. I have never heard a police service say publicly it was walking away from a problem that was its responsibility. I have heard it ask for collaborative approaches with agencies to deal with mental health or social services to try to minimize contacts with the police by people those agencies serve.

The leadership is in the language. The choice of language can undermine the best of intentions. The spirit and intent of reconciliation is acknowledgement and action. Choosing your language as a leader and remembering that people are listening to what you are saying means weighing what you are saying carefully.

In the movie *Saving Private Ryan*, a squad of men has been sent to retrieve one soldier. Following D-Day, the soldier was the only surviving brother out of four from one family. As the squad trudges inland from the invasion beaches, the soldiers assigned to the mission are complaining and griping about having to risk their lives to save one soldier. One of the soldiers asks the captain in charge of the mission why he doesn't complain. The soldier asks the captain what he would say if he was asked about the mission. The captain replies he would support it in the most positive terms. The soldier who believes the mission is futile asks why the captain would reply that way. The captain answers, "because gripes go up never down."

Every great leader I have served with understood this. I adopted and practised it. No matter how difficult things were, I never complained in front of the people working for me if I didn't have a solution to offer—a real and tangible solution, not a theory. Otherwise, I just carried on with the mission at hand. Even if the task was difficult and unpleasant, I knew as a leader there was nothing to be gained by joining negative conversations and giving them credibility. There weren't many days when I was working where I didn't say out loud at least once a day, "I love this job," or "I love this city."

Your attitude is everything when you are the leader. The language of leadership is positive and can-do around the people you lead or who look up to you. Students from a small high school in Prince Albert got it done with positive language. Surely as leaders we can do the same.

APPENDIX 2
HOW INDIGENOUS YOUTH CAN STAY OUT OF TROUBLE

Little things can start you on the path of criminal troubles and bring you into contact with the criminal justice system. If you're a young First Nations person in Canada, you already have a higher chance of contact with the police than most other young people. That is a statistical fact. The many reasons for this are more than I can put into this story, so I just want to talk about how to stay out of trouble from my experience as a First Nations man and as a former police officer.

I had to leave my hometown and live in a community eighty kilometres north of home to go to high school. There were only a couple of First Nations people living in the town; everyone else lived on a neighbouring First Nation, so I stood out. The local police would slow down when I was walking around. They would give me the long slow stare, but I never reacted. No giving them the finger or yelling, "What do you want?" They got tired of looking at me after a while.

After I joined the army, I had a couple of run-ins with the military police, but they were self-inflicted encounters arising from drinking and fighting. Unfortunately, in the infantry, those kinds of incidents were fairly common among young soldiers in the late '70s and early '80s, and I was not immune to them.

One incident that stood out, although I don't think it had anything to do with race, did teach me how it felt to be unjustly accused. We were on a winter exercise in Wainwright, Alberta, an annual event where we trained for winter warfare. We wanted to mislead the enemy force about our intentions in the maneuvers. My job was to be part of a patrol to the enemy force lines and to allow myself to be captured on purpose. Marked maps are never supposed to be carried on patrols, but some soldiers still did it. So I had a marked map showing false positions and defences to mislead our opponents. I tucked it into an inside pocket of my parka, where a searcher would really have to dig for it. Our patrol crossed over the enemy lines and after a brief firefight with blank rounds I found myself surrounded.

I surrendered and after a bit of a roughing up I was taken to the attached military police section for interrogation. I was placed in a tent, and we went through all the steps we learned in training. I gave my name, rank, and social insurance number and refused to talk. After we went through what was expected of each other, one of the military police officers told me the next portion of my interrogation was a "No Duff."

"No Duff" was a term used to indicate a real situation on a training exercise over the radio. An example would be real injuries or emergencies occurring. No Duff would clear the airwaves and take priority over all other radio traffic.

The military policeman and his partner broke out their notebooks, and the older one flipped a plastic baggie out containing three pills and held it up to my face. In an accusatory tone, he asked what they were. I had a habit of carrying multivitamins in a plastic baggie that I kept in my field message pad (a tough army notebook with a camouflage cover). I laughed and told them they were vitamins. They didn't laugh and told me they had better be. The more officious officer pressed me to admit they were something else. He would not accept they were vitamins. I was tired and less than comfortable, so I made the mistake of saying this was worse than a bad joke.

The interrogating officer turned red with anger and said they would be sending the pills for analysis and I would be charged if there was a prohibited substance in the pills. Knowing what I know now, I hope he had fun with that because it was a fair bit of paperwork to send things for analysis. I was returned to my unit the next day. I never heard anything more about the incident, and no apologies were forthcoming. It was an unnerving experience to be accused of wrongdoing out of nowhere. In retrospect, I probably could have reacted better, but the whole incident made me angry.

After the exercise, we returned to our garrison in Winnipeg and were given some time off. I was in the north end of Winnipeg with another First Nations soldier, drinking and bar-hopping in civilian clothes. We were walking down Main Street when a Winnipeg Police cruiser passed us and slowed down to look us over. My partner was a scrappy guy and he extended his middle finger and said, "Fuck you guys!" The patrol car made a U-turn and came back toward us. The car stopped right beside us, and two large police officers got out. They both looked angry and confrontational. I was intimidated, and suddenly my mouthy friend didn't seem as confident as he was a moment before. I stepped in between the officers and my friend. I told them we were soldiers and we just came back from a tough six-week exercise. We were blowing off steam and my friend had a bit too much to drink.

The officers expressed their disappointment in us as soldiers disrespecting the police. They thought our respective services shared a common bond. My friend was very contrite and after being checked for outstanding warrants we were free to go.

The whole incident could have gone several different and regrettable ways. I learned if you don't want to deal with police officers, a good place to start is not to swear at them and give them the finger when they're doing their jobs, especially in a high-crime area. Was it a race issue? It could have been, but if you are the one being profiled or street-checked, let the person doing the check raise the issue of race. If they do, you are in a much better position to have it dealt with.

Even after I started with the Saskatoon Police, loss prevention officers followed me around in stores when I was in civilian clothes. It was fun to see their faces when I returned to the store in uniform to take custody of a shoplifter. I didn't need to say a thing. The look on their faces said it all.

That being said, as an Indigenous person, I understand the anger, resentment, and frustration of being stereotyped. Our reaction to it is what will define us. The most common reaction for me was I would feel sorry for close-minded people and then try to educate them. If I couldn't educate them, I just didn't have anything more to do with them. If you are actively profiled or assaulted by a person who is racist, report it. Racists don't like being exposed. They count on people not reporting them.

I have seen good people spiral into criminality way too many times over the course of my career when they didn't have to. It can start as simply as getting a ticket for not having a licence. A person would miss their court date, for whatever reason, and have an arrest warrant issued for them. The next time they dealt with the police, they would be arrested and released with a new court date, which they would miss again. Sometimes it was because they couldn't pay the fine or they had to work or some other distraction. The next time they dealt with the police, they would be fearful because they knew they had an outstanding warrant, so they would lie about their name. They would get discovered and be charged with obstruction of a police officer for providing a false name to avoid the arrest. Now a Traffic Safety Act offence has become a criminal matter.

The spiral would continue. They would get released and, feeling they were going to jail, would miss their next court date. Another warrant would be issued, along with a new charge of failing to attend court. This time, when getting arrested, the person tries to escape and picks up a resisting arrest charge or unfortunately has marijuana. Every scenario is different, but, sadly, so many start off with something like this.

Situations like this one are especially more likely to happen to our people from northern and remote communities who have trouble getting back to the jurisdiction where the first charges were laid. So many entrances to the criminal justice system could have been avoided with knowledge and education.

When it comes to the legal system, take care of the little things and own up to what you have done. If you don't know what's going on, ask when you are dealing with law enforcement. There are some people who start big with serious offences like armed robbery and assaults. They have chosen their path and, unfortunately, it will take them where it takes them. But the vast majority of our Indigenous people who do come into conflict with the law start small and let it get out of control. Do not be that person who has to call and tell their relations they cannot come home because they are in jail.

I'll also tell you, stay in school. We are blessed in this country to have schools and education for anyone who wants it. It's free to a point, and the people in the system want you to succeed. There is no real excuse in this age for not taking advantage of this opportunity. If you can work part-time while you are in school and earn your own money, you quickly realize the value of it. I know some of our communities have rundown underfunded schools, but they are still schools. There are many Indigenous people in the world that do not even have this. If you have to leave your home community to go to school—as so many of us have had to do—use the opportunity to better yourself. Use the gym and library when you are lonely for home, because you will be lonely. But stick with the schooling—it is where your future begins.

Your generation will make it possible to have a better future for the next. If you are reading this, you are already on the right path because reading will help you in ways you have never thought of. Keep as much of your culture as you can but know the reality is you have to live in both worlds. You need to take the best traits of both and make yourself the best you can be. Listen to our storytellers and, though you might not hear the lessons at first, know that you will.

See your own value and people will see the value in you. Make the personal choice not to use drugs. No illicit drugs—except magic mushrooms—occur naturally in our country, so therefore it is not natural to put them in your body. Our communities have been decimated by opiates, cocaine, and meth. Too many funerals and lost dreams are what drugs bring to us, so make the right decision for you and your relations. Some problems seem overwhelming to us, but we can only take them on one at a time.

Be the helper, not the one in need of help. One time I stood over a young lady with another First Nations officer in an apartment who died with a needle in her arm. She was young and pretty, even in death. We were both constables at the time, so we didn't have to tell her loved ones of her death. I can still see her. We didn't know what to say to each other. I hope you will never put your families through such a thing.

Drugs bring gangs. It's their main source of income and in many ways why they exist. Resist gangs. I know some of the members are our relations, but they do nothing that makes our lives better. They can be equated to the people who eat the last of the food before the children have eaten.

Northern people know if you see a bear or wolves in the wild you avoid them so there are no misunderstandings. If you emulate gang culture in the way you dress or the music you listen to, gangs will seek you out as a potential recruit. If you don't believe the lyrics reflect who you are as a person, listen to something else. Popular culture sometimes glorifies drugs, guns, easy money, and disrespecting women. Nothing could be further from what we have been taught and told as First Nations people.

Be as self-reliant as you can and take care of your body. You don't need money to get yourself in good physical condition. You can do it wherever you are. Running, walking, and push-ups are all about motivation fuelled by personal drive. Being self-reliant means taking care of the little things, everything from cleaning up after yourself to earning a living. If you do those things, you gain self-confidence. You set an example and you are being a leader. People who are self-confident leaders rarely come into conflict with the law—they are too busy making other people's lives better.

I know some of our people feel we are over-policed and unfairly targeted. Some of our people feel the courts treat us unfairly. If you ask someone who has been the victim of crime, or fears to live in their own community because of gangs, drugs, and criminals, if they feel the same way, the answer will be quite different. If you have had trouble with the law, it's not the end of the world, but once it's resolved it should be the end of having trouble.

There are legions of academics and social justice advocates who will point out everything that is wrong and needs to be fixed. Finger pointing and blame abound in countless studies and publications about the police, First Nations, and crime. As a young First Nations person, if you don't want to become part of the text or the subject of one of these studies, avoid trouble.

I know these things sound simple. The reality can be more complex and challenging when you are trying to stay in school and avoid situations that cause the police to show up. There really is no way around keeping it simple to succeed. It takes common sense and often hard work to stay out of the criminal justice system.

You as young people need to take the lead in changing the statistics and changing the future. No one else will do it for you.

APPENDIX 3
INDIGENOUS SELF-RELIANCE AND RESILIENCE

In the past couple of years, I have had to learn how to be a civilian. No longer a police officer or a soldier, I had to wait for the news like everyone else. I get parking tickets like everyone else, and I don't carry a gun anymore. I am more reflective than reactive, and writing has given me a voice I never really used before. Some of the values I have had my whole life are firmly entrenched and some other absolutes have loosened a bit.

The first value that is firmly entrenched in my community, the Indigenous community, is the need for all of us to be as self-reliant as possible in everything we do. Self-reliance allows you to help others and to be a leader. Being self-reliant also allows you to work from a position of confidence to help change things. It also makes you less reliant on the decisions of others who may not always have your best interests in mind.

By being self-reliant and doing the little things you know need to be done, everything falls into place. So many segments of Canadian society find themselves beholden to the whims and finances of others. To be independent of reliance on outside agencies or government brings the freedom people need to succeed. The government, of course, still has influence on our day-to-day lives. Our defence, the environment, and the protection of the food chain are just a few areas where we need strong and effective leadership from our governments.

As an Indigenous person, though, I believe when it comes to band and mid-level governance, the need for effective self-government is the most pressing. We hear the stories when a band council, or chief, misappropriates money. We hear sometimes about nepotism. Stories like these are often used in the argument against self-government.

What we do not hear, however, are the many success stories from many of the First Nations across our country. First Nations and Aboriginal people have been in the news a lot lately. Many stories have a negative tone, and there is always something that seems to need fixing. But one of the things most people who read or hear the stories miss is the underlying theme of resilience in First Nations and Indigenous communities. No one is going away, nor are they folding up their tent and packing it in.

The population growth in Indigenous communities is among the highest in Canada, and many young people are taking advantage of the opportunities a completed education provides. All of these young people are making changes—some subtle, some obvious—and most of the changes are for the positive.

I was on a leadership course at the Saskatchewan Police College and one of the instructors liked quoting an American naval officer who wrote several books on leadership. The officer's approach to leadership was to ask every sailor on the ship he commanded for input on how to make his ship better. He turned the warship he was in command of from one of the lowest rated ships into the number one ship in the US fleet in less than a year. Some of the other course candidates pointed out he had a closed environment free from many outside influences, which gave him an advantage while he was making changes. Certainly, this was a factor in his success, but it doesn't take away from his achievements.

I believe First Nations leaders now and in the future will have the same unique type of environment to use as a springboard to building successful communities. There are not a lot of First Nations communities where the overwhelming majority of the population doesn't know each other because they are too big. Most First Nations communities tend to be tightly knit and have long family histories with ties to the community on all levels. As a leader, I would think this is an advantage too good to be passed up.

I understand the same advantage can also be an obstacle to a leader. Inter-family rivalries, long-standing grievances, and very different life experiences depending on the generation your band members come from all make uniting a community a challenge. Taking an inventory of where a band stands and what the community wants to achieve is always a good first step. Do we have fire protection, potable water, and a good school? Do our young people have opportunities here, or do they need to migrate outside of the community to achieve success?

The current government raised our issues extensively in the last election and, as a result, garnered one of the largest Indigenous voter turnouts in Canada's history. We have only had the right to vote for the past fifty-eight years. We should exercise that right 100 percent of the time, every time.

Now let's talk about follow-through. I have lived through many promises in my lifetime, both broken and kept. The long and short of it, motives of governments aside, is we are part of the national conversation in a lot of segments of Canadian society. More than I can ever remember. Some stories are negative, and others celebrate successes. I have said this many times before in my writing and public speaking: this is the best time to be an Indigenous person in Canada, especially for our youth.

Our young people have the opportunity to provide leadership and shape the future like never before. It comes with heavy responsibility and unique challenges. Changing a relationship with governments and a population of many other diverse cultures, while respecting everyone's rights, can look like an impossible undertaking.

The march of time has been relentless, and during this march many of the events that have affected us as First Nations people have been examined in detail. For many younger Canadians, this was the first time they heard of them. It came as a shock because many of the injustices were never taught or only briefly touched upon in schools. In fairness, human nature being what it is, I have found a lot of people—unless directly affected—take only passing interest in events that shape others.

The residential school system, the '60s Scoop, and numerous examinations of the justice systems in Canada revealed a legacy of pain and trials for all of us as Canadians. Reconciliation and sharing knowledge of these events have had long-lasting effects on First Nations communities, and it's been a good start to bringing them to the attention of the rest of Canada. Some of the remaining current issues facing us are equality in education, resource management, and the administration of justice, especially justice for the many young people affected. But there are other younger people, better educated and more vocal, who are willing to protest loudly against what they see as unjust.

What is most powerful now are well-thought-out and well-presented arguments when addressing the issues that affect us. Advancing positions on facts and evidence goes a lot further than blanket accusations and divisive language, which our neighbours in the United States indulge in a lot. We are our own people with the ability to solve our own problems. We can learn from what is happening in the United States, take the positives, disregard the negatives, and move forward.

We have many advantages the Elders did not have when it comes to finding solutions. We have human rights commissions with the power to deal with inequalities, even if it takes many years. We have a publicly funded national broadcasting company that devotes an entire website to Aboriginal issues. We have many First Nations publications and writers who are ready to address issues that affect us. The courts have tried many times to address Aboriginal issues in their decisions. If we do it right, this is the where the storytellers fifty years from now will say everything changed when telling our people's history.

When I think of the inequalities and outright attempts to exterminate or assimilate First Nations in the first two hundred years of contact with Europeans, it makes me wonder how we managed to survive as a people. Reserves, the pass system, issued rations, and all the other things we cannot even imagine nowadays—the people and governments who did this are all dead. There is no one to hate or debate. Yet we are still here. Leaner and wiser than we ever were, we are still here. As an Indigenous man, this resilience and perseverance makes me proud, as it should for all Indigenous people. Bittersweet and something to be proud of, we have endured. The time for endless debate is now for scholars and historians. It's time to move forward, acknowledging the past and suffering of our Elders, but moving forward.

One of the lasting legacies of the past, which still causes endless problems, is governance. There are a bewildering number of people in charge of our futures and not all are elected by a one person, one vote system. Consensus on issues where many different levels of governance have a stake in the outcome is very rare. From band councils and chiefs to assemblies, there are a lot of voices to unite on key issues. We double down on the confusion by bringing in or depending on the federal and provincial governments to make things happen.

I know some people will read this and say I don't know what I'm talking about. In some respects, they are right. I struggle as a layperson and nonpolitician to understand how we are governed day to day. I am not a player, just part of the discussion. But I believe in equality in education, resource sharing, and equal treatment under the law. I think the sooner all Indigenous people, from Pelican Narrows, Saskatchewan, to Halifax, Nova Scotia, fully understand how we are governed and why, the better off we will be.

For young people, learning how we are governed is something they should be taught in schools. Know the process and you can make the changes. If we do not learn this, we will be just like everyone else when it comes to who makes the decisions. Lawyers, the wealthy, and well-educated people who learned the system and then take part in it dominate Canadian politics.

If you are a young Indigenous person, now is the time to step up and fill leadership positions as they become available. Find and emulate our successful leaders, learn from others' mistakes, and take the best from all the systems to make it our own. Simplicity in execution, clarity in purpose, and honesty are leadership traits we need from our young people. We are distinct peoples who are still a part of the overall Canadian nation. No one is going anywhere, and we need to sort out who is in charge of what so there isn't a continual power struggle between governments over who is responsible. Ultimately, as young Canadian Indigenous people, you are in charge of your own success, either as leaders or those being led.

I admire resilience in all cultures. Canadians have been through four wars in the past hundred years. They have gone through the Depression, Spanish flu, TB, AIDS, recessions, and a host of other calamities. New Canadians have left ongoing wars, famine, and human rights abuses in their former countries. The underlying theme is resilience.

The most serious and potential threats to us as Canadians today are drugs, organized crime, corruption, and criminals. As Indigenous people, these are our most serious problems as well. We traditionally have different approaches to crime and punishment; finding a balance is an ongoing dilemma. We can and will find solutions if we work with everyone else to do it.

It isn't easy to believe we have made progress if you are a young person, but, believe me, things are and have been changing for all Canadians in the past thirty years. In some conversations I have had with Indigenous activists, they've adamantly stated, "I don't care about everyone else. This is about us." These are powerful words that, to me, show disconnection with traditional Indigenous inclusiveness. Sharp and rigid positions just mean you can be bypassed and ignored if you don't—or can't—demonstrate a willingness to realize there is always a bigger picture with other people who aren't going anywhere in the equation.

Proper health care and affordable education are issues for all Canadians. Equality in health care and education are huge challenges for Indigenous communities. When you add in equality in education, it becomes a unique First Nations problem. Funding levels for First Nations students have been proven to be below what the average Canadian student is receiving.

When I was working as a police officer and we were shorthanded, it was so busy we felt we would be overwhelmed by the calls for service. I would look at those challenges as opportunities to be decisive and make a difference as an individual and a leader. The problems that are right in front of us and fixable should be looked on as opportunities to lead.

Indigenous leadership faces some unique challenges, which makes providing leadership even more rewarding. When confronted with a problem (for example, water quality), there are a few questions to ask: How can we resolve this with the resources on hand? Is there a traditional solution in keeping with First Nations traditions? If not, is there a way to combine local resources, traditional methods, and nontraditional methods?

Doing something when a problem presents itself and self-reliance are strong leadership traits. Confidence and enthusiasm are contagious, especially when the person who is confident and enthusiastic has been through many trials and tribulations and still carries on. Celebrate other leaders' successes because they are successes for us all. If you take "What's in it for me?" out of your leadership, it's amazing what gets accomplished.

I'm not a head-in-the-sand type of person. I know there are many challenges for Indigenous people, especially Indigenous youth, in Canada. The Truth and Reconciliation Commission hearings brought our history forward to millions of Canadians with open minds. Issues like poverty, inadequate housing, and an epidemic of suicides would have been, at the most, local stories thirty years ago. Now they're national. When the rest of Canada hears of these challenges, fairly or unfairly, they are also looking at Indigenous leadership and asking themselves, "What are they doing?"

It is one of the consequences of being part of national conversations about Indigenous issues. Times are changing, and our successes need to be highlighted as well as the inequalities. There are bands that have addressed so many of the challenges we have heard about through effective leadership. Unless we share our stories with the same passion, their accomplishments remain local.

Shortly after leaving policing, I spoke at the First Nations University of Canada campus in Prince Albert. When I had finished, an Elder approached me and told me I was part of the start of the seventh generation. She explained some Indigenous people believed they would suffer through seven generations of trials before success and contentment returned. I have never been too traditional. I have always felt instinctively that in my lifetime Indigenous people would retrieve and rediscover their place in Canada on their own terms. But the Elder reaffirmed something I have always believed. If what she said is true, I'm honoured to be a small part of it.

For young people, it is a time of opportunity, a chance to lead and shape the future. It just makes sense to want to be part of it.

WILLIAM HAMILTON, HAMILTON PHOTOGRAPHICS

Ernie Louttit, a member of the Missanabie Cree First Nation, was born in Ontario and raised in Oba, a small village 1,000 kilometres north of Toronto. Ernie started working on the railway when he was 15, and at 17 (as soon as he was able) he enlisted in the Canadian Armed Forces. Once in the army, he joined Princess Patricia's Canadian Light Infantry, where he rose to the rank of master corporal. Among other missions, he served as a UN peacekeeper. After a stint as a military policeman, he was hired in the late 1980s by the Saskatoon Police Service, only the third Indigenous officer in the force's history. He spent more than two decades in uniform patrolling the city's streets and ended his career as a sergeant. Much of his police work was in Saskatoon's inner city, and during that time he proudly bore the nickname given him by local residents, "Indian Ernie." Post-career, he has written three books on his life experiences, including this one. His earlier works *Indian Ernie: Perspectives on Leadership and Policing* and *More Indian Ernie: Insights from the Streets* have become bestsellers. Ernie is also a busy motivational speaker who targets Indigenous youth with a message focused on leadership, tolerance and empathy.